THE DOUBLE-CROSS SYSTEM

in the War of 1939 to 1945

THE DOUBLE-CROSS SYSTEM

IN THE WAR OF 1939 TO 1945

BY J. C. MASTERMAN

NEW HAVEN AND LONDON: YALE UNIVERSITY PRESS, 1972

To the Earl of Swinton, P.C., G.B.E., C.H., M.C., D.L.,
amongst whose many services to Great Britain
the Chairmanship of Security Executive 1940-42
was not the least.

Designed by Sally Sullivan
and set in Linotype Times Roman type.
Printed in the United States of America by
The Carl Purington Rollins Printing-Office
of the Yale University Press.

Distributed in Great Britain, Europe, and Africa by
Yale University Press, Ltd., London; in Canada by
McGill-Queen's University Press, Montreal; in Latin
America by Kaiman & Polon, Inc., New York City;
in India by UBS Publishers'
Distributors Pvt., Ltd., Delhi; in Japan by
John Weatherhill, Inc., Tokyo.

CONTENTS

FOREWORD

Sir John Masterman's account of the double-cross system in British intelligence is an important historical document. Masterman is a trained historian and is well aware that he is describing a chapter of World War II which deserves being known and remembered. Masterman is also a skilled narrator. *The Double-Cross System in the War of 1939 to 1945* is an engrossing book as well as a highly serious one.

There is no need to vouch for the authenticity of the episodes and cases he describes of spies who worked ostensibly for the Germans but, in fact, and unknown to the Germans, were working for Great Britain. The official origin of *The Double-Cross System* is sufficient affidavit. Nevertheless I can endorse their authenticity, having been aware of many of the cases in connection with my own war work. My particular counterespionage affiliation was with M.I.6. This was the British agency responsible for intelligence operations outside the United Kingdom; the "Military Intelligence" of its name was an anachronism. B.1.A, which handled the counterespionage operations Masterman describes, was a section of M.I.5, the British internal security agency roughly equivalent to the American F.B.I. What went on within the United Kingdom was, properly enough, Great Britain's affair. But those enemy spies who were uncovered there and persuaded to work for the British from then on, thus double-crossing their original masters, of course had ultimate contacts outside of the country. Thus the cooperation of M.I.6 and its opposite numbers in Allied intelligence services was inevitably involved.

Viewed in retrospect, certain British contributions to the

art of intelligence operations seem outstanding. In the field of interception the results were splendid and increasingly dominant, as the many published accounts certify. The techniques of intercepting messages sent by wireless were highly developed. So was the science of direction-finding by which the location of the transmitting instrument could be determined. By the constant monitoring of all wireless traffic of any sort it was possible to check not only what the double agent sent out, if he was his own wireless operator as he usually was, but also messages sent to him. It was possible too, by careful study, to evaluate the critical reception by the enemy of what they received and exchanged amongst themselves. This was the test of any plan of deception. Not the least of course among the benefits was the simple fact that the existence of new spies became known. In this way both the skeleton and the nervous system of German espionage within England could be outlined and controlled.

Another contribution was that of so-called overt intelligence, by which scholarly sources, when studied by scholars, revealed information which had long since been gathered but already been covered by dust. Timetables for tides involved in invasion landings, the location of bombing targets within metropolitan areas, amounts of precipitation to provide against and rainy seasons to avoid: these not-at-all trivial data emerged from the otherwise ignored pages of books rather than from the impossibly delayed reports of agents. American intelligence services learned much from the British example of research and analysis carried on at the universities. But the double-cross system was of course not itself involved.

Certainly the most imaginatively appealing success of British intelligence work was the operation of double agents, and through them the practice of deception. The center of this activity was in the B Division of M.I.5. At least it was the center of what Masterman describes. For as he states, this was an activity which involved many branches: M.I.5, M.I.6, the Admiralty, the Air Force, the Home Office, and the Foreign Office, among others.

As in World War I, the British government partly by necessity, partly by design, drew on the universities and the professions for additional brains. Amateurs joined hands with professionals in the intelligence establishment. Work with double agents was a game made for one amateur— J. C. Masterman—who was a university don and an enthusiastic cricketer. His mind was tuned to the pitch of the ball in this sport whose hazards were so real and whose rewards were so immense. This was the greatest test match of the century. It is by no mere rhetorical flourish that Masterman can refer to two masters of cricket when he remarks of two masterly double agents, "If in the double-cross world SNOW was the W. G. Grace of the early period, then GARBO was certainly the Bradman of the later years." Skills were involved in the double-cross game, and absolute coordination. The British were masters and whatever Americans did similarly in the European and Mediterranean theaters stemmed from British direction and example.

The sense of example which *The Double-Cross System* provides gives the book a particular merit. It is a manual of operation. There has never been one like it. When Americans midway in World War II were preparing for their own external counterespionage system, its novices were given, half desperately, Compton Mackenzie's *Water on the Brain* (1933). Manuals on either espionage or counterespionage are after all rare. Graham Greene's satiric *Our Man in Havana* (1958) is perhaps as good as most. Edward Weismiller's novel *The Serpent Sleeping* (1962) is one of the few accounts of the handling and psychology of a turned agent, in this case after the invasion of France, when German agents attempted to operate behind the American lines.

Lieutenant Commander Ewen Montagu's *The Man Who Never Was* (1953) is the most famous account of strategic deception and the most detailed. Duff Cooper in his novel *Operation Heartbreak* (1950) had told the story earlier, but Montagu, as a member of Naval Intelligence, was a chief begetter and the case officer of this completest of deceptions. By means of false messages found on a body, itself a concocted corpse, washed up on the Spanish coast, the Germans were persuaded that the next Allied invasion in the Mediterranean was to be in Sardinia rather than in Sicily, where it actually took place. The German high command was successfully deceived.

Lord Ismay, chief of staff to Winston Churchill as minister of defense, gave Montagu's book a semi-official blessing by writing an introduction to it. "It is not often," he said, "that the whole story of a secret operation can be made public, told by someone who knows every detail. The military student can be grateful that chance has made it possible for him to have a textbook example of a very specialized branch of the art of war: others will enjoy a 'real-life thriller' —which once more illustrates that truth is stranger than fiction." Lord Ismay was indicating, in advance, the values similarly to be found in *The Double-Cross System*.

Masterman is no stranger either to truth or fiction, as his deservedly popular mystery stories witness. The shrewdness of *An Oxford Tragedy* (1933) may even have played a part in drafting him for the "XX" (translated as "Twenty") Committee whose task was to pass on and manage the complex manipulation of double agents. This involved the supervision of whatever the double agents sent in the way of volunteered information or as answers to questionnaires, and involved equally the attempt to build the agents up for the moment when each could play a more decisive role. These moments did come, as when the Normandy invasion was shielded by diverting the enemy's attention to the likelihood of a Norwegian landing. They came, too, when it was important to confuse the Germans on the success of their missile bombing of London by the V-1s and the V-2s. The British double-cross system was responsible for the saving of hundreds and thousands of lives. Both truth and fiction played parts.

The element of "game" was, as I have said, fortunately not absent. A sense of freshness was kept. "For the plain truth is," Masterman writes in his introduction to *Fate Cannot Harm Me* (1935), "that breaking rules is fun, and

the middle-aged and respectable have in this regard a capacity for innocent enjoyment at least as great as that of
the youthful and rebellious." Some of the amateurs in B.1.A
were no doubt "middle-aged and respectable," but their
enjoyment was by no means "innocent." Masterman's postwar novel, *The Case of the Four Friends* (1957), he calls
in its subtitle "a diversion in predetection." The tale is a
conversation about guilt. "Let me try to explain," a guest in
the Senior Common Room of an Oxford college says about
the shadiest of the four friends:

> Portugal was neutral, and so to Portugal came the agents
> official and unofficial of many countries and countries
> on both sides. It was not possible to learn in Berlin what
> was happening in London, but it might well be possible to
> hear, or guess, or deduce in neutral Portugal what was
> happening in both. And further, it might be possible to
> spread information (and make it appear credible) of
> what was *not* happening in London or Berlin and yet have
> it believed in the other place. And so Lisbon became a
> kind of international clearing-ground, a busy ant-heap of
> spies and agents, where political and military secrets and
> information—true and false, but mainly false—were
> bought and sold and where men's brains were pitted
> against each other. There was, of course, more in it than
> this. The life of the secret agent is dangerous enough, but
> the life of the double agent is infinitely more precarious.
> If anyone balances on a swinging tight-rope it is he, and
> a single slip must send him crashing to destruction. Ban-
> nister went to Lisbon ostensibly in a commercial capacity,
> and he was well-known and respected in British and
> allied diplomatic and business circles—but he was much
> more than that.

Bannister was indeed "much more than that." So were all
agents. The conversations about Bannister and his friends
in the novel sound very much like those in which members
of the Twenty Committee and their colleagues might have

bandied the probabilities and possibilities of a SNOW or a CELERY.

The creed of the Twenty Committee is given explicitly in Masterman's text. It is worth repeated reading:

1. To control the enemy system, or as much of it as we could get our hands on
2. To catch fresh spies when they appeared
3. To gain knowledge of the personalities and methods of the German Secret Service
4. To obtain information about the code and cypher work of the German Service
5. To get evidence of enemy plans and intentions from the questions asked by them
6. To influence enemy plans by the answers sent to the enemy
7. To deceive the enemy about our plans and intentions

Carefully Masterman traces the achievement of these objectives. The question was not simply one of locating a spy and then arresting him. Masterman's committee had no executive power, and if it had had such power, would have used it only sparingly. Any counterespionage agency respects the enemy and recognizes that the elimination of one operation only spurs the enemy to replace it by another. For that reason it is often better to watch a known agent than to seize him, and to controvert his utility by denying him access to important intelligence and by supplying him with what was known as "chicken feed." Best of all, of course, is to persuade the spy, by one means or another, to work instead for you. One is not frightened of an "enemy's" or a "friend's" intelligence service so long as it is gelded. Not the least accomplishment of the double-cross system was such surgery.

Happily and with justice Masterman could claim for the British double-cross system that "for the greater part of the war we did much more than practise a large-scale deception through double agents: by means of the double-agent system we *actively ran and controlled the German espionage system in this country.*" The italics are understandably his. Once

the war was concluded one of the first Allied objectives was
to check the German intelligence records to see what if
anything had been missed or misplayed. There was no reason
for British confidence to be shaken so far as the Germans
were concerned. It is the English story which Masterman
tells and uses as precept and primer. Accounts drawn from
German sources seem to tell another version of their espionage within England. They are proof of the deception.

Masterman's report is a fascinating one. It is authori-
tative and it satisfies one's curiosity. He outlines the development from the early period when the British were on the
defensive and were protecting themselves against the probable invasion of England. This was the age of SNOW. Later
came the phase when the initiative was beginning to pass
to the Allies, and there was in the foreseeable future a probable invasion of the Continent. Then GARBO led off. The
enemy were watching the change too. The double-agent
system which had been built up for the first phase was
recycled for the second. The shift was delicate and dangerous. Like a good tutor, Masterman never loses control of
history in his report, "in order," as he puts it, "that the main
course of the story may not be delayed or interrupted." Yet
his contemporary concern was far more than narrative; to
those on the Twenty Committee the story was always continuing, always changing, and must always be controlled.

Masterman gives us a world of stratagems, inhabited by
characters like SNOW, like MUTT and JEFF, like TATE and
ZIGZAG and TRICYCLE. They were known only by these
cover names and in them they lived and operated. But
each life was shared. "It cannot be too strongly insisted,"
Masterman out of experience asserts, "that the most profitable cases were those in which the case officer had introduced
himself most completely into the skin of the agent." Nuance
became all. Even the methods of communication between
the agent and the enemy, whether by wireless, by secret
writing, or by personal contact in neutral countries, required
empathy on the part of the case officer and the planners. The
details of a man's wireless style, for example, the warning

signals, the very rhythm of the key in sending messages must be mastered so that if the agent should die or for one reason or another be removed, a substitution could be made but not recognized. The dermal and subdermal took on new and nerve-wracking significance.

The Double-Cross System is not the only document to describe double agents and deception. It is simply the best. In some cases Masterman's story can be interestingly amplified, as in Montagu's description of Operation MINCEMEAT and "the man who never was." The same sort of amplification can be done, though less confidently, with Eddie Chapman's own account of himself as ZIGZAG, the saboteur (he was known as FRITZCHEN to his German employers), in *The Eddie Chapman Story* (1954).

What is significant in *The Double-Cross System* is the system itself. In a philosophical sense it is the "game" which counts. Certainly it was what counted for the soldier who splashed ashore on Sicily or in Normandy. Behind the "man who never was" were dozens of conscientious and clever men who were. Masterman describes their work. These were the ecologists of double agency: everything was interrelated, everything must be kept in balance. Yet in the end there was an enemy to be induced down the wrong path, wrong for them but right for us. Fortunately they went.

New Haven   Norman Holmes Pearson
September 1971

PREFACE

This book was written during the months of July–September 1945. At that time I had been participating in double-cross work for four and a half years. On 7 July I went on fifty-six days release leave and my final release came on 1 September, a couple of weeks before the book was completed. These dates have some importance; my service was in fact over but I was asked by the Director General of the Security Service and by his deputy to write a report of double-cross work during the war. Accordingly I stayed in the office and had access to all the relevant documents; but the report differs somewhat from what it would have been had I been still a serving officer when I completed it. In particular I allowed myself to state with clarity what I thought of primary importance with regard to the future of secret intelligence organizations. I do not know what effect, if any, my last chapter had on those in authority. Possibly it had none, for few of them can have read it. But I am conscious that I felt entirely uninhibited when I wrote the report. Any value which it may have stems in my view from the fact that it was written in 1945. A history of double cross commissioned a few years later would have become to a great extent a *livre de circonstance* or a piece of propaganda; written in 1945 it was a report, coupled with my own observations and comments on secret intelligence work. For this reason the story is now published in the form in which it was printed (though for a very restricted circulation) in September 1945, with only a few excisions and verbal amendments.

The book, then, was written as a report and there was in 1945 no thought of publication at all. As time passed, however, it occurred to me and to others who knew of the book that there might well be a case for publication. As the secrets of the war years were revealed the objections to publication steadily diminished, for it can now be argued that nothing which could be of value to a potential enemy is revealed which is not already known.

As objections to publication diminished, the case for publication gained in strength. I felt that if security objections were removed, there was no decisive argument against allowing people to read reliable accounts of events which had taken place. It was also right to give credit for a successful operation to those who deserved it—in this case M.I.5 and, to a lesser extent, M.I.6. This I took to be important because the general opinion of the Secret Service was low. Any good work done by the Secret Service is usually unknown except to those in high places and those personally concerned. On the other hand any error or partial failure receives a great deal of publicity and a spate of criticism. Failures are exaggerated, successes are never mentioned. Some of the spy cases of the fifties and sixties, for example, have seriously damaged, usually unfairly, the image of the Secret Service. Although this is inevitable, it carries with it unhappy consequences, for when reputations suffer, confidence in the services is lost. As Hugh Gaitskell put it in 1961, "Secrecy may be essential but confidence must be restored."

Even before 1961 it had seemed to me that publication of the double-cross story might help in some small way to restore confidence, for it is after all a success story, and one which could be told without impinging on other counter-espionage work. Here a point must be made. It has been said that the success of the Service during the war was due to the recruitment of "amateurs" from outside and that after the war the Service relapsed into a state of inefficiency—to use no harsher term. On this point I must confine myself strictly to what I know, or rather what I knew in 1945, for I was myself one of the "amateurs" and I can speak with the experience of more than four years of observation. I do not know what may be the truth with regard to other departments and sections in the Secret Service, but I do know what was the case in that section which controlled the double-cross agents. We, the amateurs, contributed (I like to think) some useful ideas, and we formed a loyal and efficient support for the professionals. But it was the professional officers of M.I.5 who were responsible for the policy, for the plans, and for their execution, and who provided the initiative and the leadership which the rest of us needed. To the professionals, therefore, the credit for the success of double-cross work should go. I believe too that, to use the favorite phrase of all military appreciations, "lessons to be learned" showed beyond doubt that cooperation between different departments and different services was the one essential condition for success. This cooperation was more evident in the double-cross business than in many other spheres.

Arguments of this kind led me to propose some years ago that the double-cross story should be published, but it became evident after consultations that my proposals were premature. Now, a quarter of a century after the end of the war, it has been decided that the story may be published. The permission of Her Majesty's Government has been given, and I am grateful.

To avoid misunderstanding another point must be made. Though the facts are for the most part not in dispute, the views and theories propounded are my own, and I alone accept the responsibility for them. Certainly some of them, and perhaps many, would not receive the complete or unanimous support of others concerned in double-cross activities. Nevertheless it has, for obvious reasons of convenience, been necessary to use the word "we" freely throughout the text. Roughly speaking, where the personal affairs of the agents are concerned, "we" stands for the B.1.A section of M.I.5 (Military Intelligence 5 is the Security Service, B.1.A that section of it which dealt with the double agents); where matters of policy are at issue, "we" connotes B.1.A supported by the Twenty Committee—so called from the moment of its first meeting because the number twenty written in Roman numerals represents double cross—as well as, in important matters, by higher authority in M.I.5 and by the W. Board. Where speculative theories and views are advanced, "we" is only the cover name for myself.

Oxford   J. C. M.
September 1971

LIST OF ABBREVIATIONS

A.A.	Antiaircraft
A.D.C.	Aide-de-Camp
A.T.S.	(Women's) Auxiliary Territorial Service
B.U.F.	British Union of Fascists
C.	Head of M.I.6
D.B.	Director of B Branch of M.I.5
D.D.N.I.	Deputy Director of Naval Intelligence
D.G.S.S.	Director General Secret Service
D.M.I.	Director of Military Intelligence
D.N.I.	Director of Naval Intelligence
D. of I.	Director of Intelligence (Royal Air Force)
F.S.P.	Field Security Police
G.H.Q.	General Headquarters
H.E.	High Explosives
J.I.C.	Joint Intelligence Committee
M.A.	Military Attaché
M.O.I.	Ministry of Information
N.A.A.F.I.	Navy, Army, and Air Force Institutes
N.I.D.	Naval Intelligence Department
O.K.W.	Ober Kommando Wehrmacht
P.W.E.	Political Warfare Executive
S.O.E.	Special Operations Executive
W. Branch	Wireless Branch

1: THE THEORY AND PRACTICE
OF DOUBLE CROSS

The use of double agents in time of war is a time-honoured method both of deception and of counterespionage. They have been used frequently and extensively in most wars and in many places; they will quite certainly be used again. Every spy who is sent into enemy territory or across the lines must be alive to the possibility of capture and, in the event of capture, of saving his life not merely by full confession but by returning with messages couched in a form approved and perhaps dictated by his captors.

The high-souled fanatic may repudiate even the suggestion that he would be capable of giving way to pressure and of acting as a double agent, but the majority of spies are not of this Spartan breed, and many, perhaps a majority, of them are ready and even willing to commit treachery either under pressure or for simple reasons of self-preservation. There are, too, certain persons who are genuinely anxious to serve the side against which circumstances have induced them to operate temporarily; there are others who have a natural predilection to live in that curious world of espionage and deceit, and who attach themselves with equal facility to one side or the other, so long as their craving for adventure of a rather macabre type is satisfied. Again there are some who are ready to play with both sides at the same time and who—whilst they feel no moral objection to deceiving both sides—yet appear to maintain a kind of professional pride which compels them to render reasonably good service to each; and finally there are cases in which the spy is caught, interrogated, and executed or imprisoned but in which messages purporting to come from him are still transmitted by his captors to their enemies. The spy "being dead, yet speaketh." There is even the entirely fictitious double agent, the "notional" double agent who never exists at all save in the minds or imagination of those who have invented him and those who believe him. In short there are many different types of double agent, and they in their turn can be and have been used for many different purposes.

Granted the antiquity of the practice and the ubiquity of its application, it is still true that the manner in which it has been used in this war has presented some novel features. In the older military books the use of double agents would be mentioned as a *ruse de guerre*, for previously, so far as we know, a double agent has been used for some specific and usually only temporary purpose, e.g., for the carrying out of a single piece of tactical deception or for the transmission of a false piece of political information. But during the present war the use of double agents has been notably extended and developed; agents have been run on a long-term basis, that is to say, the advantages which may be expected from them have been postponed in order that they may be substantial, and the reputation of agents with the enemy has been carefully built up over a long period in order that when the time comes they can be used with confidence and boldness. Here particularly a great deal of judgment has been necessary. A man who invests money at bottom prices in a gold mine with a shady past history and a very dubious future may well be tempted to take a small and quick profit by selling out if the shares rise—but he will only make a fortune if he risks total loss by hanging on to his shares. With double agents we have, as it were, held shares in a great many mines, and some of them, on which we have in the early stages expended labour and money lavishly, have indeed turned out to be El Dorados. Others of course have yielded nothing and cost much; but you cannot expect in any case to draw a fortune unless you pay in, and pay in freely, first.

Not only have double agents been run on a long time basis but they have been run so extensively that we can think not in terms of a number of isolated cases but in terms of a double agent system. In fact by virtue of this system for the greater part of the war we did much more than practise a large-scale deception through double agents; by means of the double agent system *we actively ran and controlled the German espionage system in this country.* This is at first blush a staggering claim and one which in the nature of things could not be advanced until late in the history of the war. Even after we felt sure that it was in fact justified we took the greatest care not to assert it, lest the bubble of premature confidence should be pricked by unexpected events. Nevertheless it is true, and was true for the greater part of the war. Everything that follows is designed to show how this state of affairs came into being, how it was used, what successes were achieved through it, and what opportunities were missed of using it more thoroughly and more effectively. In addition we shall try to explain the principles of controlling and running double agents which have been evolved empirically, in order that advantage may be taken of this experience in the future.

Here, however, three warnings are necessary. In the first place most of these principles and rules of conduct were worked out at a time when we could not bring ourselves to believe that we did in fact control the German system. Innumerable precautions had to be taken with every agent and indeed with every message on the assumption (which later turned out to be false) that the Germans had several and perhaps many independent agents of whom we had no knowledge, and that these agents' reports could be used to check the reports of our own controlled agents.* Only long experience taught us the extent to which the Germans de-

*We had some reason for our fears. HITTITE, who was recruited by the German consul in New Orleans, was told that he would be approached by a German contact in the Regent Palace Hotel if he ordered late breakfasts there before the end of November 1940. If after three days no approach had been made he was to go to the Cumberland instead. Whoever approached him would give him full instructions and facilities.

pended upon our controlled agents and taught us too the
gullibility and the inefficiency of some branches of the
Abwehr. Beyond question opportunities were wasted and
chances missed by a pardonable excess of caution. Had we
realised from the start that the Germans did *not* draw from
other sources in this country we could have acted more
boldly and offered a better service than we did, particularly
in the sphere of deception.

Nevertheless the precautions taken were not without their
use, and the principles of running double agents which were
dictated by that caution may well have a validity in the
future. For the second warning is this: It cannot be expected that in a future war we shall have the same or even
comparable advantages. This time we had a combination
of circumstances of quite extraordinary good fortune. Circumstances, aided by German miscalculation or absence of
foresight, so fell out that the bulk of the German intelligence
system in this country fell into our lap and secret sources
permitted us to observe that the reports of our double-cross
agents were transmitted to Berlin; that they were believed;
and that competing reports were not (except those of OSTRO
and some others which are alluded to in chapter 10) equally
efficacious. Such a combination of auspicious circumstances
will surely not occur again. History never repeats itself, and
it can safely be assumed that the running of double agents
in the next war will be more difficult and more hazardous
than it has been in this.

The third warning which should be kept in mind is a
natural corollary of the first two. The methods evolved for
controlling double agents must be regarded as illustrations
and guides to conduct and not as fixed principles or invari-
able rules. The circumstances on the next occasion, whatever they may be, will certainly be quite different. Once
more it must be repeated that history does not, and indeed
cannot repeat itself, but we can learn from experience if
we are ready to adapt that experience to changed conditions.
A single illustration will suffice. The problem of communications with agents, whether straight agents or double-cross

agents, has been radically altered in this war by the use of wireless; and, whereas in the last war censorship and the British intelligence service abroad were the chief source of information for counterespionage, in this war wireless intercepts have taken the first place. A superficial observer might well spring to the conclusion that all other methods of communication—e.g. personal contact or secret writing—were out of date and of no importance for future operations. A reasonable faith in the progress of technical scientific invention might suggest that a transmitter could be made small enough to defy detection, and that codes could be constructed which it would be impossible to break. The speed and reliability of wireless communication would then cause all other methods of communication to be abandoned. Such a view, however, would in all probability turn out to be fallacious. The history of wireless transmissions in the realm of espionage is likely to be another chapter in the age-long story of the struggle between attack and defence. The old battleship is rendered helpless by the new shell; the new battleship is protected by impenetrable armour; a new explosive smashes the impenetrable armour, and so forth.* So in the case of illicit wireless transmissions. It may well be that direction finding may be developed to such a degree of efficiency that the spy or agent in the next war may be unable to transmit in safety even with the most perfect transmitter, and may therefore fall back on some other method of communication—possibly a method of which, up to now, we have no knowledge.

All this is surmise, but it is patent that we cannot expect conditions in the next war to be at a par with those in this. During the present war double agents have made their communications by personal contact in neutral countries, by secret writing (aided by microphotography), and by wireless; and of these wireless has been the most important. We cannot tell what methods of communication will be most effective in the future, but it is tolerably certain that,

*What, it may be asked, is the answer to the atomic bomb?

whatever they are, they will not be the same as those used today. In consequence much of the detailed description of double agent cases in this war can only have an academic or historical interest and much of it can be omitted without loss. There remains a residuum, interesting perhaps in itself and useful for the future by way of illustration or as a guide to future method.

We return to the main argument, that is to the claim that during the war we did actively control the German intelligence system in this country—a claim which should be confined to the period after the fall of France in 1940, when Great Britain was effectively cut off from easy communication with the Continent, up to the return of the British armies to France in 1944. The possibility of controlling the German intelligence system in fact depended upon the virtual cutting off of this country from the Continent in May to June, 1940. Prior to that date there was so much coming and going that it would have been presumptuous to suggest that we controlled even a large part of the German system. An agent who worked for us in later years told us—and the facts were easily substantiated—that he, a German, had visited England from the Low Countries in the early part of 1940 in order to negotiate with regard to the sale of a patent bandage. The fact that such a visit was accomplished without undue difficulty indicates that spies could be, and perhaps were, introduced into the country at that time. After June 1940 entry was only possible, except by illegitimate routes, through Sweden or Portugal, and the narrowness of the bottlenecks made it comparatively easy to exclude unwanted visitors or to find a concealed goat among the sheep. That was an ordinary security task of no great difficulty.

After the reconquest of France and Belgium a considerable traffic was soon restarted between Great Britain and the Continent, and he would be a bold man who would swear that no spies slipped through among the rest. It is true that our own security measures had by that time reached a very high degree of efficiency, but the complications raised by the numbers and nationalities involved made it next door to impossible to be sure that all the holes were stopped.

What exactly does the claim to have controlled the German system in England entail? German information about England must have come mainly from six sources: aerial reconnaissance, wireless intercepts, examination of prisoners of war, previous knowledge acquired before 1940 and checked from the contemporary press, neutral embassies and legations, and finally the reports of agents. It is this last source which we, through the double agent system, claim to have controlled, and it is a part, and not an unimportant part, of the whole. Now clearly if the Germans were to have information at all through agents it was preferable that those agents should be controlled rather than uncontrolled. Even if we were unable to send over any false information for fear of detection by other methods (e.g. by aerial reconnaissance), we should at least know what the Germans were receiving—and that in itself is a great gain. The haunting fear that the enemy might have accurate and detailed knowledge of some intended operation was replaced by the certainty that they had or had not such knowledge. Of course there is much to be said for aiming at the ideal of denying *all* information to the enemy. This is after all the primary object of a security service. But experience seems to show, and certainly theory would suggest, that you cannot thus deny all information and keep all activities, preparations, and undertakings secret. On the other hand you can control one of the enemy's main sources of information, and thus know what his information is, and, to go a step further, you can select his information for him, you can pervert his information, you can misinform him, and, eventually, actively deceive him as to your intentions.

Let us for a moment imagine that we stand in the middle period of the war with the double agent system in full working order, and that we have to make a case to show the advantage of the system and the benefits accruing from it. Such a case might well be summarised as follows:

1. Our prime object is to control the German espionage system in this country. The placing, establishment, and running of agents is a difficult and laborious task, and it can be assumed that if the Germans are receiving an adequate service of news from our controlled agents they will not expend a great deal of time and effort to establish another system as well. This is the chief counter-espionage advantage, and it seems to be more effective than the policy of attempting to suppress all enemy agents.

2. Our controlled agents will help us to contact and to apprehend new agents and spies. Though all espionage theory is against letting one agent know about others it remains true that new spies are often given a contact to be used in case of necessity. Spies caught in the early days of the war had often been given a lifeline of this kind, and the lifeline almost always turned out to be one of our already controlled men.

3. We obtain information about the personalities and working methods of the German service, and this knowledge is of the highest importance for counterespionage purposes. Since we know how our controlled agents have been trained, what sort of story they have been told to put up, and how they have been equipped, we are in a position to trip up and expose other enemy agents when they appear.

4. We get information about the code and cypher procedure of the enemy.

5. We gain evidence of the enemy's intentions. The questions asked must give a great deal of accurate and important information about enemy intentions; they will not ask a number of questions about the defence of southeast England if they intend to invade in the southwest. Equally the cessation of all questions about ground and beach defences is a clear indication that invasion projects have been abandoned.

6. With proper support and adequate preparation we can in some instances not only learn about but also influence

and perhaps change the operational intentions of the enemy. Thus information to the effect that our aerodromes are imperfectly defended may induce the enemy to attack them rather than factories or installations. In the same way an insidious method of propaganda can be used. Thus in 1943 BRONX, answering questions about preparations for gas warfare in England, gave a glowing account of the excellence of British preparations, and implied that gas warfare would be of greater advantage to the British than to the Germans.

7. Finally we are in a position to deceive the enemy. Clearly the necessity of sending information carries with it the power of sending misinformation, though it must be remembered that the force of this depends upon the reputation of the sender and that a long period of truthful reporting is usually a necessary preliminary for the passing over of the lie.

These advantages are palpably great, but it is obvious that a price must be paid for them, and, as the last paragraph suggests, the greater the advantage the greater the price. A double agent cannot be summoned from the vasty deep and set upon the stage ready at once to play a leading part. On the contrary, he must be steadily and cautiously "built up" in reputation, and that is a process which lasts always for months and often for years. In other words, for the period of his novitiate he is not an asset but a liability. An examination of subsequent chapters will show how this process has been carried out in a variety of cases; for the present it suffices to stress the obvious truth that the larger the prize the higher must also be the preliminary stake.

In point of fact, however, the price paid has usually not been so very great after all, for many cases have been firmly established without giving away anything especially secret or important. Still the price does depend upon the status of the agent, upon the degree of confidence which he inspires, and upon the importance of the assignment which is given to him. In any case he must be built up gradually and with discrimination and always with careful regard to what the Germans expect or believe he would be capable of obtaining. This process implies that he must communicate a great deal of true information: but who is to decide what he may be allowed to divulge? Quite clearly M.I.5 is unfitted to decide such questions. An agent, for example, is asked for information about a certain aircraft; he has had preliminary training in aeronautical matters; he is so placed that the information or part of it would, on the German view, be readily available to him; he cannot ignore the question without destroying his whole case—in other words an answer of some sort is unavoidable. On the other hand he must not give to the enemy information so valuable that it would be likely to outweigh any subsequent benefits which might accrue through him. A nice assessment of profit and loss has to be made in every case, and such an assessment can only be made by the cooperation of those who have intimate knowledge of the agent's potentialities with those who have technical knowledge of the subject of the question.

The solution of the difficulty was found in the creation, in January 1941, of the Twenty Committee (technically a subcommittee of the W. Board) which held weekly meetings from then until May 1945. The essential purpose of the Committee was to decide what information could safely be allowed to pass to the Germans, and what could not—in other words to assess the probable gain of a proposed release against the loss involved in supplying a particular piece of information to the enemy. Secondly, the Committee acted as a clearing-house where the work of the various agents could be compared and kept within a reasonable measure of consistency. Obviously contradictions in traffic of too glaring a nature had to be avoided. If we assume that the enemy studies and uses the traffic of a variety of agents we must also assume that he will distrust A or B or both if they contradict each other on easily ascertainable or important facts; *a fortiori* he will distrust and probably abandon an agent whose information is contradicted by information obtained from some other more credible source, whether it be air reconnaissance, newspaper articles, or prisoners' reports. On the other hand the reports of the agents must not bear too close a resemblance to one another. Thirdly, the Committee could compare the needs of different departments and if necessary reconcile those of one with another.

It followed as a direct result of this that a truly formidable work of coordination, preparation, and critical analysis had to be undertaken by B.1.A if the traffic of agents was to be maintained over a long period without giving away the agent to the enemy. As was pointed out above, our "lifeline," on which we kept a firm grip throughout, was the principle that no message should ever go to the enemy which had not been approved by the competent authority through the medium of the Twenty Committee. It was also pointed out that M.I.5 could, in the nature of things, not perform this function itself. How could it give the exact location of an aircraft factory which might be bombed in the following week, and then expect to be allowed to continue to run its agents? It will readily be believed that the ultimate responsibility for allowing any message to pass to the enemy is a dangerous power. In communicating with the enemy almost from day to day in time of war we were playing with dynamite, and the game would have been impossible unless "approving authorities" had been willing to assume this ultimate responsibility. Our experience was that this responsibility ought to be taken on as high a level as possible. In the period under review it was taken by the W. Board, i.e., by the Directors of Intelligence reinforced by other members, and exercised through their representatives on the Twenty Committee. On any lower level action would have been impossible, and it is arguable that, at least when the deception period began, some still higher single authority, acting directly for the Chiefs of Staff, should have had an overriding power to approve or veto all traffic and even, perhaps, to insist upon, the sending of messages regarded as essential by him.

Palpably all this could not have been done by M.I.5

either alone or even at the request of other departments, and yet it seems clear that M.I.5 is the best department to run double agents in this country, and indeed, in our view at least, the only authority which could run them effectively and successfully. This assertion needs some explanation and substantiation. In the first place, it cannot be too strongly stressed that the running of double agents in wartime demands the close cooperation of many departments, and complete confidence between them, or rather between their representatives on what may be described as a working level. There is in fact a great deal of coordination to be done, and this can best be done by a department such as M.I.5, which is to a great extent impartial in its views of the demands of other, and particularly service, departments. Next it becomes clear, the more individual cases are studied, that double agents can only be run by a department which has made some study of the German Secret Service, since any other department will inevitably commit errors of a practical kind in the working of the agents due to a lack of knowledge of the personalities, methods, and peculiarities of the other side. Furthermore, M.I.5 is primarily responsible for security and for counterespionage in this country, and the counterespionage aspects of double agent work are best kept in the foreground by a department whose interests lie in that sphere of activity. Any other department is too easily led astray by the dazzling prizes offered by deception.

In fact deception through double agents, as experience shows, is best carried out by agents who have been carefully built up and used also for counterespionage purposes. If they were developed entirely for purposes of deception, it is almost certain that they would be used too soon and "blown" in order to gain some temporary or short time advantage. Any naval officer, for example, would press hotly for the immediate use of an agent at whatever risk, if such use promised additional safety for a British ship or the possible destruction of an enemy submarine. Equally any officer of M.I.5, who had built up and controlled an agent over a long period of time, would resist the sacrifice of that agent unless the maximum benefit was extracted from the case.

On balance it appears that the best agents for deception on a high level are long-distance agents, who have been carefully built up, and who have served a long apprenticeship before any major deception is attempted through them. One has only to consider the possible alternatives to come to the conclusion that, in this country at least, M.I.5 is the body best qualified to run a double agent system. The service departments are really ruled out by their own special and closely defined interests. An agent may, for example, come to this country with an assignment of work covering matters of naval, military, and air interest. If any one of these departments was in control, it is hardly to be supposed that it would not concentrate on that part of the assignment which dealt with its own special commitments. Almost all agents are given a field of work wider than they can cover. Almost all tend, as times goes on, to show themselves more and more adept in one particular line. In other words a judicious management can lead or coax an agent into that particular sphere of activity where his services are most needed.

Nor again could M.I.6 easily take the place of M.I.5 in this particular work. The function of M.I.6 is primarily espionage, or the obtaining of accurate information from the enemy by means of spies or agents. Now undoubtedly double agents afford admirable opportunities for obtaining intelligence information, but they perform many other tasks as well. It is highly probable that M.I.6, like the service departments, would wish to take a quick and positive bonus from a case which, if used with maximum efficiency, should be developed over a long period of time and used for purposes ultimately more rewarding than the mere acquisition of information about the enemy. It has happened on various occasions, and notably in one instance of transcendent importance, that the situation has so developed that a double agent case has appeared to offer so much immediate advantage by the penetration of the enemy's organisation and by the acquisition of intelligence from it, that the double agent side of the case has been dropped in order to obtain the proffered benefits. Alas! the reflection of the bone in the water is only a reflection after all. In the instance referred to, some considerable intelligence harvest was reaped for a very short period, but a double agent case was lost, and lost at a time when it had immense possibilities particularly for the implementation of D Day deception.

So much for the theoretical aspect. More strongly still practical considerations have determined that M.I.5 alone is the appropriate department for running the system. For the running and control of double agents is a very long, laborious, and infinitely complicated task. It could not be done as a parergon by any intelligence department elsewhere; it could only be done by M.I.5 because M.I.5 was both willing and in a position to allot a whole section of officers with the necessary secretaries and assistants to this task, and to this task alone. A fuller analysis of the practical working of B.1.A, the section involved, will be found in chapter 4; for the time being it is sufficient to indicate the nature of this working.

What must here be stressed is the overriding importance of having a section wholly and exclusively devoted to this special work, and not dependent upon any one specialised department. The first advantage which B.1.A enjoyed derived directly from its position as a part of M.I.5. A double agent in many cases arrives in this country in an irregular manner, and nothing can be done with him until his position is regularised. But this process presents many and often considerable difficulties. He must be landed or refused leave to land; he must be provided with an identity card for use here, and with documents, ration cards, and clothes coupons; he must be housed, and he must be guarded or at least watched. In short a complete life must be arranged for him, and a story which will prevent the curious from poking their noses too closely into his affairs, or from spreading about him rumours and insinuations which, once started, can seldom be suppressed. All this entails work, and in the early days of a case both speed and efficiency. It can only be done effectively by a department such as M.I.5, which is accustomed to close collaboration with, among others, the police, Scotland Yard, the Home Office, and the Registrar General.

Moreover, since much of the work is secret, and since publicity spoils all, the methods used in establishing a double agent must of necessity be often clandestine and always discreet. Nor is the establishing of an agent the end of the matter. Take the simple case of a parachutist who is willing to desert his German masters and work for us. Such a man may well need the whole time service of a case officer to control and organise him, a wireless operator to monitor and perhaps to transmit his messages, at least two guards since no one can be on duty for twenty-four hours in a day, possibly an officer with a car to collect his information, and probably a housekeeper to look after and feed the whole party. Any ordinary government department would boggle at such a commitment; inevitable questions of establishment would arise, and indeed a secret department alone could undertake such responsibilities.

The administrative problems connected with double agents are formidable enough in all conscience. They become almost overwhelming when it is remembered that at any moment two or three cases may collapse, leaving personnel unemployed, or, worse still, two or three new cases may suddenly appear demanding trained staff to cope with them. Financial problems alone would make it impossible for a straightforward (if the word may be used without offence to anyone!) department to undertake the control of a double agent system. It is true that in the long run the enemy have usually paid for the services provided, but it is also true that at times money has to be spent freely and quickly and in an imaginative manner. The actual cash supplied by the Germans to maintain their and our system between 1940 and 1945 was something in the region of £85,000. Economists may wrangle about the benefit or loss accruing to us from this return of currency to the country, but at least the sum indicates the value set by the Germans on their agents' reports, and offers a reasonable excuse for B.1.A expenditure.

The further the analysis is carried, the more self-evident does it become that a double-agent system in wartime can only be run by a large section of a secret, or partly secret, department, highly trained and exclusively devoted to this specialised work. It was mentioned in an earlier paragraph that heavy responsibilities must be shouldered by high-ranking officers in other departments; it must now be added that these officers must also be educated up to their responsibilities. We must teach our masters, and this can only be done by a section fully apprised of all double agent information, and deeply impressed by the many-sided advantages of the work. Furthermore much has to be done in deciding the policy to be followed, both in selecting and running cases. Many apparently promising cases have had to be rejected because of circumstances outside our control. An agent, at the description of whom the collective mouth of B.1.A would water, may have to be rejected at once, simply because too many talkative persons were present at his capture or acquainted with him in an earlier existence. Others again have to be run for a time because it is impossible at the start, to know whether they will be useful or not. Such experiments, though they often fail, must be tried because the reward for success is great. But all cases, successful or unsuccessful, demand work and time and application from many people, and the reserves in manpower are far from being unlimited.

It will become obvious in the subsequent chapters how nearly some of the most fruitful cases were to being discarded as hopeless in their early stages. Fortunately for B.1.A it will never be known how many cases potentially of great value were either never started or abandoned because of unexpected hitches or because of the competing claims of other cases. Studying the luxuriant prose of GARBO or the terse and virile telegraphese of TATE, one may speculate a little sadly on the "mute inglorious Miltons," who may have languished at Ham or even at Lisbon because they could not find a publisher for their work or even a literary agent to put them in touch with a publisher.

In the course of these operations B.1.A worked out certain principles in dealing with double agents—or perhaps it would be truer to say that, in the course of the work, certain principles became apparent. For the purpose of convenience some of these principles are enumerated here; a study of the cases would show them in clearer relief:

1. First and before all it is a cardinal principle that no traffic of any kind should ever be sent over without the written approval of some competent authority. This point has been sufficiently explained already.
2. Double agents, provided the preliminary investigations show good hopes of success, should usually be accepted and used when occasion offers, but they should *not* be created. If a person offered himself and could satisfy us that he had in fact been approached and recruited by the Germans, he could probably be used with advantage. On the other hand when we tried to throw an agent in the way of the Germans with a view to persuading them to recruit him, we almost always failed. This rather curious fact was in some ways the most important practical lesson which we learned in the theory of double-cross work. Cases occurred in which an individual appeared to have been specially designed by providence to become a double agent. Imagine an Englishman who has spent much of his early life in Germany, and who has business interests and relatives in that country; suppose too that he has real reason to dislike the British government—he may, for example, have been cashiered from the army or sentenced in the courts for some illegal transaction, or he may have become attached to some fascist organisation in time of peace; in spite of all this he has ostensibly remained a loyal British subject. Such a man, it might be sup-

posed, has only to be encouraged to appear in a neutral
country for the Germans to attempt to recruit him. In
point of fact, such a bait was rarely taken. "Coat-
trailing" was usually a failure.

That was irritating no doubt, but the picture had its
bright side. Though they would not take a first-rate
article from us, the Germans showed themselves more
than willing to push a second-rate article of their own.
Indeed their childlike belief in the value and importance
of some of their own agents was sometimes so thorough
and persistent as to strain credibility. It appeared that
the only quality which the German spy-master demanded was that he should himself have discovered
the agent and launched him on his career. There is a
reason, of course. The system in the Abwehr was that
any member could start and control an agent. Not
unnaturally the prestige, and presumably the income,
of many Abwehr personalities depended upon the reputation of their own particular agents. If then the reliability of a double agent was questioned by the enemy,
his chief defender always turned out to be his own
spy-master, who would go to almost any lengths to
protect him against the doubt and criticisms of rival
persons or of Berlin.

Incidentally this flaw in the German system which
we observed fairly early in the history of the war suggests a weakness in our own system. With us, it is true,
all agents were controlled centrally; but nonetheless, a
zealous case officer was apt to become obsessed with
the importance and impeccability of his own cases and
to be, for the best of motives, unwilling to subordinate
them to the general interest. It may well be that in the
next war the Germans will work on a better system.
Be this as it may, the principle still holds good that
cases should be accepted when they occur, but they
should not be artificially created. The principle does
not of course apply to notional agents, who are in a
different category.

3. The next principle is that a double agent should, as far as possible, actually live the life and go through all the motions of a genuine agent. If, for example, our agent was told by his German masters to inspect and report on factories at Wolverhampton, we arranged, if it was possible, that he should visit the place himself before he replied. If he could not go a substitute was sent in his place. The agent on such a journey sought information exactly as a spy would, that is to say, with the most intense regard for his own safety, and in consequence he secured the sort of account which a genuine spy would have got. As a result his messages appeared to be true, and he did not trip over details of topographical or local observation.

The principle of verisimilitude was kept up in other matters also. For example, if an agent had notionally a subagent or cut-out in the country, he ought actually to have had and to have met such a man. If this was not done, he would almost inevitably break down under examination if, at a later stage, he met his German masters in a neutral country—since no one can hope to memorise and be infallible with regard to a lengthy and wholly fictitious tale. If an agent were asked for a personal description of his subagent, he would answer more readily and be able to avoid mistakes, if he had an actual living person in his mind's eye.

No one can study the interrogations of agents sent by the Germans through the escape routes without realising the imperative necessity of making the agent actually experience all that he professes to have done. A spy who alleges that he escaped through France and Spain to England may start his concocted story with spirit and confidence, but if he has not actually trudged along the escape route, he will very quickly flounder into difficulties and discrepancies which no ingenuity can long disguise. "And then you come to the little river," say the interrogator, "tell me about the ferry there, and what sort of man rowed you across?" The victim describes the ferry to the best of his inventive power, and so, all unconscious that he should have said "There was no ferry. I walked across the bridge," plunges to his inevitable doom. To embark on an early lie is fatal, for an early lie can never be caught up.

Broadly speaking, then, this particular principle amounts to little more than an insistence on the prime necessity for truth whenever truth is possible. A lie when it is needed will only be believed if it rests on a firm foundation of previous truth. As a corollary to this it is also desirable that the agent, if he is to be highly esteemed, should obey the instructions of his German masters as nearly as may be. He will not carry weight if he transfers his interest from, say, a study of convoys to the manufacture of aeroplane engines. But within the limits of his instructions he should take the initiative, since thus and thus only could he cause those questions to be asked which we were prepared to answer, rather than those which we would fain have avoided. An agent who found himself hard pressed by detailed questions about troop concentrations in his own district of East Anglia could sometimes escape by informing the Germans that he had heard rumours of important troop movements in Scotland and suggesting that he should visit that locality to find out. The Germans could seldom resist such a fly if it was accurately and skillfully cast. In other words the initiative had to be retained because a passive and defensive policy was certain in time to lead either to trouble or to the collapse of the case.

Further, the retention of the initiative implied both a far-sighted and a foreseeing control. It is impossible at a moment's notice to move an agent plausibly to an area whence a cover plan has to be implemented; it is comparatively easy to arrange the agent's notional life so that his business should demand his tranference from Southampton to Aberdeen in April with a view to passing over important information in August. But here again difficulties arose. In the nature of things plans and cover plans were not and could not be agreed and fixed far in advance; circumstances might change them and events might hasten or retard them. It was therefore necessary, if the agent were to be rightly placed and firmly established at the crucial moment, to guess the course of events and to guess them correctly. For deception purposes the whole issue might be put in one sentence: "Can you when D Day comes (and we cannot tell you when that will be) be sure to have your trusted agents (guaranteed trusted by the Germans as much as by you) firmly established in those parts of the country where they can be most effective (and we cannot tell you when that will be) be sure to have your trusted the agents, therefore, we had always to keep several moves in advance of the game, planning always for an uncertain future, and hoping at least to guess rightly more often than we guessed wrongly.

4. The fourth cardinal principle in the system which was developed was that a case officer should be assigned to each double-cross case. It is essential that every agent should be run and controlled from day to day by an officer who knows every detail of his case. It is impossible, especially in the case of agents working by wireless who must needs give some answers quickly, to deal adequately with many questions unless there is someone who knows exactly what has happened throughout the case and who, therefore, knows at once the relevance of certain questions and their relation to what has gone before. The case officer must, as it were, live the case with the agent. He must be in a position to say "X ought to scream for money this week; three weeks ago he said he had only £20 left," or "I am sure that X would make a great point of his information about these tanks at Guildford. Remember that he had special training in identification of tanks, and what a good mark he got last January for a similar piece of information." The organisation dealt with

many agents; only by having case officers could we be reasonably sure that any one case was not temporarily neglected because others were boiling over—and if neglected even for a short time a case might well be irretrievably ruined.

The case officer then had to identify himself with his case; he had to see with the eyes and hear with the ears of his agent; he had to suffer himself the nervous prostration which might follow an unusually dangerous piece of espionage; he had to rejoice with his whole heart at the praise bestowed by the Germans for a successful stroke. It cannot be too strongly insisted that the most profitable cases were those in which the case officer had introduced himself most completely into the skin of the agent. The best and most ingenious suggestions for the development of a case came usually from a case officer.

Nonetheless, as was indicated above, a real danger is implicit in this method. What is best for the case is not necessarily best for the double-cross system as a whole, and sacrifices had sometimes to be made in the general interest which ran counter to the hopes and the views of the particular case officer concerned. It would seem right, if a future war calls for the reestablishment of a double-cross system, that the policy in every case should be determined by those in charge of the section, who would of course obtain detailed knowledge of the case from the case officer. It is also important that no case officer should be overburdened with too many cases. Probably in more than one instance cases have gone awry, or have failed to start at all, simply because the case officer was fully occupied at the moment by a crisis in one of his other cases. Experience seems to show that no officer should ever handle more than two cases of major importance at the same time, and ideally he should never have more than one. If he has, in consequence, lengthy periods of comparative leisure, he can usefully make himself acquainted with other cases, both for purposes of comparison and in order that he may—at need—take over a case from some other officer.

5. Closely linked with this principle is the next, i.e., that a most careful psychological study must be made of each agent. This was done partly by the case officer, partly by the head of the section, and its importance is best seen by remembering once more that double agents work for very varied reasons. Thus an agent who has decided to turn round in order to save his neck may well, after some months, feel that his conduct has been despicable, and that he would rather suffer death than continue to collaborate. He must be carefully studied and watched so that he does not go bad on us unexpectedly. The agent's collaboration may at times be absolutely essential. One agent, for example, had questions asked of him about the distribution of an estate left by his deceased grandmother. Had he not been by that time giving us his genuine assistance, the case must have been blown sky-high by our inability to deal with this personal matter and our want of knowledge about the deserts and reliability of various lawyers and relatives. On the other hand the messages sent mentioning the different characters in this domestic affair must have increased German confidence in the *bona fides* of the agent.

On the whole it was found well worth while to attempt the gradual conversion of such characters from the principles of the totalitarian state to a better way of thinking, for their active assistance could be of great value. An agent taking interest in his traffic was capable of making the most useful suggestions and criticisms and was worth far more than one working under compulsion and against the grain. Still more was this principle of importance in the case of agents who were genuinely on our side but conscious of the dangers run by their families and dependents, and still more acutely conscious of their own merits and of the risks they were running for the common cause. In their cases every idiosyncrasy had to be studied and their demands, even if extravagant, satisfied as far as possible —otherwise they would never give the fullest and most useful service of which they were capable. Every double-cross agent is prone to be vain, moody, and introspective, and therefore idleness, which begets brooding, should be of all things the most carefully avoided. Give any agent plenty of work "that an empty stomach do not feed upon humour." Generally speaking an actual job, altogether apart from espionage, should be found for every agent.

In considering the psychological approach to agents the propaganda value of converting them to a better way of thinking should not be entirely neglected. It is commonly said that double-cross work has nothing to do, and should have nothing to do, with propaganda, but this generalisation cannot be accepted without reservation. On a long-term view nothing helps a country more than generous and humane treatment of prisoners of war. Almost every prisoner who is well treated becomes to a greater or less degree an advocate of the country of his captivity. In the same way the conversion even of a handful of Nazi agents will not be without its beneficial effects. But even more their reports on morale in this country and reports on the effects of bombing or of secret weapons *must* have a certain, and probably a considerable, effect upon those who receive the reports. A considered and planned attempt to persuade their people of the determination of Great Britain to pursue the war to a complete and final victory might well in certain circumstances have hastened their realisation that they had lost the war.

Unfortunately in this war the prestige of the Abwehr was clearly low, and the advice of the Abwehr had probably very little weight. But an Abwehr of the future might be more highly regarded and its influence on policy much greater, and in that case the propaganda use of agents and their reports would have to be taken into account. For that purpose our relations with Political Warfare Executive (P.W.E.), or its equivalent would need to be closer and more intimate than they were in this war. Wherever the fault may have lain—and it was probably ours—it is difficult to avoid the conclusion that we did not do all that we might have done serving as a weapon of political warfare.

6. The next principle is that a fixed and generous financial agreement should be made whenever possible with each agent and that this agreement should be made as early as possible. When agents were working voluntarily, it was found advisable to let them share on a percentage basis in the money received from the Germans, especially when large sums were involved. The incentive provided by such prizes was often sufficient to stimulate the agent to increased effort and to increase the value of his suggestions and proposals. The agent who is not treated generously is apt to become disgruntled, especially when he observes large sums coming to us through his instrumentality. But it should not be forgotten that the agent could receive no money at all unless we were running the case, and he should therefore be taught from the beginning that all incomings belong in right and in fact to us, but that to reward him for his collaboration we are prepared to give him his percentage. Fortunately in this war the Germans paid highly enough to make a double-cross system practically self-supporting, besides providing us, according to the sum offered, with a rough and ready but generally reliable criterion of the trust which they reposed in any particular agent.

7. The next principle is that of decisive and rapid action at the start of a case, even at some considerable risk. The need for such rapidity of action is self-evident, for it is not to be supposed that the Germans will lend credence to an agent who delays for some weeks to

make contact with them and provides no reasonable explanation of the delay. But unfortunately in this matter the principles of right conduct are difficult to reconcile with one another. Almost all unwilling or doubtful agents tend to keep back part of their story and much of their information, presumably in order to have cards up their sleeves to play if the game takes an unexpected turn. It is therefore often fatal to start a case until a thorough and systematic account has been obtained of the agent's history, background, ante-cedents, and connections with the Germans—otherwise he will probably (perhaps even according to his own plan) be betrayed by his early messages. He may for example have a warning signal which he will not dis-close until he has convinced himself that we are really better friends to him than the Germans are ever likely to be. We had also to find out, in the case of a wireless agent, whether during his training the Germans became familiar with, and took records of, his style, for if they had, he had to operate the key himself. Even if his style was not recorded it was usually best to allow the agent to construct his own messages, since idio-syncrasies of style and wording are easily recognised though not easily reproduced.

It was also necessary to obtain at the earliest pos-sible opportunity an accurate and detailed account of the agent's life from his earliest years, since this account almost certainly contained traces of other personalities with whom we were acquainted, and because any devi-ations from the truth would almost certainly be detected sooner or later. The greater the detail into which an agent goes, the more certainly will he trip himself up if he strays into falsehood. And again, the greater our knowledge of the agent's past the easier it is to avoid errors and personal inconsistencies in his messages.

From this point of view, then, no agent should be allowed, in theory, to start until his whole story has been sifted and corrected and his whole past examined. In practice such thorough preliminary work is of course impossible, and a balance must be struck between the rival principles of safety and speed. Generally speaking a risk had to be taken and the agent started on his career as soon as it was fairly certain that we had the main lines of his story. But to avoid error it is wise to change his messages in nonessentials, e.g., in the manner of dating and order and choice of words, so that an unexpected warning signal may be avoided. Fortunately enough the Germans did not as a rule provide really sound equipment; probably no German agent in the early days would have made contact without the technical assistance of our wireless experts. It was consequently often easy to get one message across and then simulate a breakdown, thus gaining the necessary interval for further researches into the agent's history.

It may be noted that the difficulties mentioned above do not have the same importance in the case of letter-writers, since letters can be antedated in order to provide a longer period of investigation before the letter is actually written and despatched. Incidentally this very real difficulty of reconciling a quick start with the need of obtaining a complete story before the start is made militated against the success of double agents recruited in the field or in liberated countries.

8. It is a commonplace of counterespionage work that success comes and spies are caught not through the exercise of genius or even through the detective's flair for obscure clues, but by means of the patient and laborious study of records. In the case of double agents it is equally true that only a most careful and minute record of each case can save the case officer or the directing officers of the section from committing— sooner or later—some blunder with regard to the agent. No one can remember with exactitude what was said or inferred six months previously, and only a well-kept record can save the agent from blunders which may

"blow" him or inconsistencies which will create suspicion. The actual traffic which passes between the
agent and the enemy must be kept as a matter of course,
and must be constantly studied, but in addition a record
must be kept of conversations, journeys, and actions,
so that the notional story may acquire substance and
wear the appearance of truth.

It is probable, in a review of the cases concerned,
that in this war we erred on the side of overelaboration
and excess in our files. Too often the essential features
of a case were buried under a mass of irrelevant and
redundant detail. Possibly the file or files of each case
should be reviewed at intervals, and the unnecessary
documents destroyed or replaced by a short note. It is
only necessary to point to the thirty-five volumes in
the SNOW file or the fifty-odd volumes connected with
GARBO and his affairs to make clear the enormous difficulty of mastering the essentials of such cases in a
reasonable space of time and with some degree of
certainty that no essential feature has been overlooked.

9. The next principle is one which is almost universally
respected in espionage work. It is that every agent
should as far as possible be kept clear and independent
of other agents. In putting this principle into effect we
usually had the collaboration of the Germans themselves, and also of the agents. A spy is naturally nervous
of any contact which he does not make himself, and the
Germans had a proper dislike of crossing lines unneces-
sarily. From our point of view it was important that if
one double agent was "blown" for some reason which
we could not forsee, he should not bring down others
with him in his fall. Moreover, it was sometimes necessary to risk an agent for some specific purpose, but this
became difficult if failure entailed not only the loss of
that agent but also of others whom we had allowed to
be tied up with him. Nevertheless it was not always
possible wholly to avoid connection between individual
agents. Much though he distrusts connections, the spy

often has his morale improved by being given some one address to which he can appeal if a real crisis occurs in his affairs. In particular he is often given someone to whom he is to go if his money fails. Not uncommonly one double agent was given the address of another who would supply him with funds if he urgently needed them. This sort of tie-up cannot be altogether avoided without creating suspicion, but it is a firm rule that it should be agreed to only when it must.

10. The degree of risk which should be taken in double agent cases is a controversial question. To what extent can untruth and misinformation be passed over without endangering an agent? Obviously no precise answer can be given to a question of this kind, but experience has clearly and incontrovertibly shown that we erred in the direction of overcaution. Naturally at a time when we were compelled to consider the possibility of real and undiscovered agents in this country acting as a check on reports sent by us it was impossible to risk very much falsehood, but as confidence grew in the inability of the Germans to secure other evidence, we could and should have taken greater risks. The fact that we have so many facts and details under review makes it obvious to *us* that a certain message if sent *ought* to blow an agent. But in truth it probably or almost certainly will not; and for this there are many reasons.

In the first place the agent reports to his spy-master in the first instance, and the latter in his turn sends on the information to higher authority, often without examining it in close detail. If the error or risk is one of a discrepancy or contradiction, it is highly unlikely that the higher authority will have the detailed knowledge of the case necessary to observe it. It may well be that the actual source of the report will not even be reported, since the spy-master may be anxious to gain prestige for himself and may be running "notional" as well as real agents. If, however, the higher authority does grow suspicious, it is the spy-master who will go to the last extremes, for reasons both of prestige and personal profit, in the defence of his agent.

Nor again does a message necessarily bear the same damning interpretation to the Germans as it does to us. The single instance of Norwegian deception will suffice to illustrate this. We assisted on many occasions in creating the threat of an invasion of Norway from this country; we started always with the belief that the agent might succeed but must "blow" himself in the process. Such was not the case. An agent has to report facts if he can. He reports the concentration of troops, the collection of landing craft and the like in the appropriate areas; the Germans believe that the invasion is imminent and make their dispositions accordingly. But when the deception succeeded the agent was *not*, in our experience, usually "blown," for the Germans had far more credible explanations of what had occurred than the true explanation that the agent was a double cross. They thought that he had been misled and had exaggerated what he had seen; they thought that the plan had been adopted but had been later abandoned; most likely of all they thought that the honest agent had been himself deceived by the British cover plan. The landing craft which he sedulously observed and most properly reported were indeed *in situ*, but he could not be expected to discover that they were in fact dummy craft. His reputation for truthful reporting was well established, and it was far more reasonable to suppose that he had been misled by the British than that he had over a period of years tricked and deceived his German paymasters.

In short it was extremely, almost fantastically, difficult to "blow" a well-established agent. On one occasion an agent was deliberately run in order to show the Germans that he was under control, the object being to give them a false idea of our methods of running such an agent and thus to convince them that the other agents were genuine. The theory was sound and the gaffes committed were crass and blatant, but the object was not achieved, for the simple reason that the Germans continued to think of the agent as being genuine and reliable!

The difficulty of blowing an agent suggests another rule of conduct: Never in running a double agent commit an irrevocable act if this can possibly be avoided, because you cannot predict what the future will be. In almost every case there came a moment or moments when we were tempted to commit an irrevocable act, that is to say an act which, in return for some temporary advantage or merely to get rid of an apparently unsatisfactory case, would shatter the case beyond hope of recovery. In such circumstances it almost invariably turned out to be right to refrain from decisive action; sooner or later, if no irrevocable act had been committed, the case revived, probably in a manner not expected by us.

It must not be forgotten that the Germans were working with uncertain data and acting on information imperfectly understood by us. We might be tempted to think that an Abwehr officer "Y," studying his records, must realise that agent "X" was suspect. We were apt to forget all the minor factors which might alter the situation, as, for example, the posting of "Y" to Russia, or the destruction of his records by bombing, or even the mere inefficiency of himself or his subordinates. The wisdom of refraining from the irrevocable act is one of the most important principles evolved in working agents, but to pursue this course demands patience, confidence, and willingness to face the criticism of lack of initiative. "If I hear people saying that something must be done," said Lord Melbourne on one occasion, "I know that they contemplate doing something damn silly." To refrain from action with regard to these cases at a doubtful moment was not always easy, but it turned out to be almost invariably right.

11. Another principle which was worked out was that, at a time when suitable double agents were numerous, due regard should be paid to quality as against quantity. In a sense this principle is self-evident, for it is plainly impossible, when the number of case officers is limited, to take on an excessive number of cases. Nor, though many cases cause confusion and doubt in the enemy's mind, can it be denied that too many cases tend to reduce the practical effects produced by any one of them. But on insisting on quality—that is on high-grade agents—we have to be clear what we mean by "high-grade." It is a mistake to suppose that the well-placed person friendly, let us say, with a Cabinet Minister or an official in the Foreign Office or a highly-placed staff officer is necessarily in the highest grade of agents. The indiscreet remarks of ministers or generals do not carry much conviction, and it is a truism of historical research that when dealing with diplomatic conversations and the rumours of embassies we are in the very realm of lies. The German staff officer needed facts, for with facts before him he could make his own appreciations. So it is certainly true that it was of far more value to him to learn, for example, that a certain division had moved to the area of one of the northern ports, or that it had had instruction in mountain warfare, or that it had been issued with arctic equipment, than it was for him to hear that "Lord So-and-So in the Cabinet told me in the utmost confidence that an invasion of northern Norway was being discussed by the Chiefs of Staff."

It follows from this that the highest-grade agent is often a low-grade man. A seaman or a wireless operator can give much more useful information with regard to convoys than the most expert or well-informed spy of the traditional pattern. In grading a double agent, therefore, we have to consider two things; is he really trusted by the Germans, and is he in a position plausibly to provide them with facts even if those facts are confined to a very limited field? An agent may be in the highest class for reliability and may be wholly trusted, yet he may be also wholly unable to secure useful information without straining credibility to breaking point. *Per contra* he may be so placed that he can plausibly obtain high-grade information and even very high-grade technical information, but he may not be trusted by the enemy and is therefore useless. An agent of high quality we must attempt to establish firmly in both ways.

12. Finally, and only in the later stages of the war, a new principle acquired some measure of credence amongst us. It was this: that, whilst for most purposes the most genuine agent—i.e. the one who kept nearest to truth— was generally the best, for deception "notional" or imaginary agents were on the whole preferable. This theory received its greatest support from the case of GARBO which is described in chapter 9 and following.

So much for the general principles of double-cross work, and for the lessons which have been learned in running a double-cross system. It remains to outline the arrangement of the chapters which follow:

Chapter 2 describes the origins of the double-cross system immediately before the war, and the working of the system during the "phoney" war. Chapter 3 contains an account of the arrangements made by the Germans to reinforce their agents here in the autumn of 1940. Chapter 4 is concerned with the organisation devised here to cope with and control the double-cross system. Chapter 5 gives an account of the traffic of the agents during 1941. Chapter 6 describes the experimental plans and deceptions carried out during that year. Chapter 7 covers the personal history of the agents in the same period. Chapter 8 deals with the development of the system during 1942, especially in the sphere of deception.

Chapter 9 deals with the work and history of the agents in 1942. Chapter 10 is a summary account of the activities of 1943. Chapter 11 describes the use of double-cross agents for deception covering the Normandy landings and the invasion of France. Chapter 12 covers the work of the agents in the last year of the war. Chapter 13 offers some concluding remarks.

This introduction should end with a confession of faith. If war, in Clausewitz's phrase, is "a mere continuation of policy by other means," it is equally true that peace is unfortunately often only a condition of latent war. Counter-espionage must be a continuous process, an activity which persists in time of peace as well as in time of war. But it is not, and never can be, certain against whom counter-espionage may have to be directed in a few years' time. As Lord Rosebery once wrote, "foreign policy necessarily varies with the varying importance of states. There is, indeed, no such thing as a traditional foreign policy in the sense of its being necessary and inevitable, any more than in all conditions of the atmosphere a ship carries the same traditional sails, or a man wears the same traditional clothes." The only safe rule of conduct would seem to be that we are fully entitled to adopt counterespionage measures against any power which indulges in espionage, whether that power be for the time friend or foe.

No counterespionage service, however well organised and however efficient, can hope to prevent all espionage, but it can keep its controlling finger on all espionage and be ready to strike at it at any moment. It is a commonplace that the most effective policeman is the man who has the most reliable informants, and American experience is said to show that in crushing illegal organisations those forces of law and order have had most success which have themselves had links with the underworld. To tackle enemy espionage (whoever the enemy may turn out to be) it is therefore of paramount importance to keep a firm hold on the enemy's own system of agents and informers. Knowledge of his methods, knowledge of his intentions, and knowledge of the personnel of his organisation are all vitally necessary. Surely all these objects are best attained by the maintenance of double agents! The confession of faith is consequently a simple one. It amounts to this: that in peace as well as in war a carefully cultivated double agent system is the safest and surest weapon of counterespionage, and the one most easily adaptable to changing conditions, changing problems, and even changing enemies.

2: ORIGINS OF THE DOUBLE-CROSS SYSTEM

On 5 May 1939, a member of the Deuxième Bureau gave a lecture to certain officers of M.I.6 on the value of "double-crossing agents" from the counterespionage point of view. He stressed specially the importance of penetrating the enemy Secret Service, and of discovering enemy intentions, and incidentally painted a gloomy picture of the preparations already made by German agents in France armed with "absolutely indetectable" wireless sets, in the use of which they had previously been trained. He gave also—if the brief note of the lecture can be trusted—some rather rudimentary advice with regard to the practical handling of double agents.

In fact the warnings and the advice were both superfluous, for M.I.5 and M.I.6 were already alive to the value of such agents and were actually working them before the war began. Moreover, in July 1939 the Directors of Intelligence recognised the importance of double agents. Of these the earliest and the most important was SNOW, and it is proper, therefore, that any history of double agents during the war should start with him. From him much was learned of importance about the Abwehr and its methods, and in addition we gained contact with German espionage, put our fingers on several German agents of less importance, and built round him the foundation of a double-cross system. He was in fact the *fons et origo* of all our activities for the next five years.

The history of SNOW is interesting and at times melodramatic. He was an electrical engineer who had emigrated at an early age to Canada. He returned to England a few years before the war and took up employment with a firm which was the holder of a number of Admiralty contracts. During this period of his life SNOW travelled frequently to Germany on business, and was in the habit of bringing back a certain amount of technical information which he passed to the Admiralty.

At the beginning of 1936 SNOW told his contact there that he would like to work regularly for the government, and was therefore passed on, through D.D.N.I., to M.I.6, who employed him for a short while as an agent, apparently with good results. Towards the end of the year, however, a letter from SNOW to postbox 629, Hamburg, a known German cover address, was intercepted in transit. This letter made it clear that SNOW had been previously in contact with the Germans and was about to have a meeting with them at Cologne. This appointment he kept, and further letters were observed to pass between him and the Germans. No action was taken against SNOW himself, as it was anticipated that he might presently confess. In December he did in fact do so and told the following story.

SNOW said that his business had brought him into contact with a German engineer named Pieper, from whom he had attempted to obtain information. The information which Pieper had supplied had not been wholly satisfactory, and after a while SNOW had found himself unable to continue to pay Pieper's expenses. At this point Pieper had proposed to him that he, SNOW, should work as an agent for the Germans rather than the British. SNOW had fallen in with this suggestion in order, so he said, to penetrate the German Secret Service in the British interest. Pieper had accordingly arranged meetings for him with the Germans at Cologne and elsewhere, and SNOW had been accepted by them as an agent.

It is still not clear to what extent SNOW's confession was tendentious. It can, however, be stated that he must have been recruited by the Germans in much the way that he described, and at some date after he had become an agent of M.I.6. There can be little doubt that the Germans were aware of his connection with M.I.6, though according to

Snow himself they believed him to have broken off this connection before he took service with them. At all events they did not subsequently make any attempt to employ him in the capacity of a double agent, but rather to use him as a straightforward reporting agent. As there were some difficulties in the way of proceeding against Snow on account of his previous connection with M.I.6, no action was taken against him, and he continued his association with the Germans. A great part, however, though not all, of his correspondence continued to be intercepted, and from time to time Snow himself gave information either to M.I.6 or to Special Branch about the contacts which he had made with the Germans and the information which he was being asked to supply.

Substantially from the end of 1936 until the outbreak of war, Snow worked as a straightforward German agent, whose activities, although known to the authorities, were not interfered with in any important respect. Snow's principal contact in Germany was Major Ritter, alias Dr. Rantzau, who has since become familiar in a great number of cases, both here and in America. During the time that Snow knew him he appeared to occupy the position of the Leiter of I. Luft, Hamburg,* and Snow's work, therefore, consisted largely of collecting air force information. From time to time, however, as is clear from his correspondence, he supplied information both for the naval and the military sections in Hamburg. At one moment also he seems to have made an approach on the Germans' behalf to the B.U.F., to whom he put forward a scheme for the establishment of four secret transmitters in England for the purpose of disseminating propaganda in time of war. This must presumably have

---

*The Abwehr, the German Secret Service, was divided into four principal departments or Abteilungen: Abt Z, a general administrative department; Abt I, espionage; Abt II, sabotage; Abt III, counterespionage and security. Abt I was further divided into sections responsible for obtaining a particular type of information. There were I Heer, I Marine, I Luft, I Technik Luftwaffe, and I Wirtschaft. The organisation of subordinate stations, or Abwehrstellen, throughout Europe reflected the organisation of the Abwehr as a whole.

been a function of Abteilung II, and it can therefore be said that during the three years between 1936 and 1939 SNOW was in reality acting in England as a kind of one-man Stelle. Although we cannot be certain on this point, it seems from his own account that SNOW successfully represented to the Germans that he possessed a number of subagents in England, amounting perhaps to a dozen or fifteen men. It is probable, though not certain, that all these persons existed only in SNOW's imagination.

In January 1939 SNOW informed Special Branch that he expected to receive a wireless transmitter from Germany. Later in the same month he did receive a letter which contained instructions for the working of such a set and a ticket from the cloakroom at Victoria Station, where the wireless set had been deposited for him in a suitcase. This set was handed over by SNOW to Special Branch and examined by M.I.6, and then returned to him. He installed it in his own house and attempted to establish wireless communication with Hamburg. It appears from his correspondence, however, that he did not succeed, as the result apparently of some defect in the set itself.

In August 1939 SNOW left England for Hamburg together with an Englishwoman of German extraction with whom he subsequently lived. He also took with him an individual whom he clearly intended to recruit for the German service. They returned at the end of August and for a short time disappeared completely. On 4 September, however, SNOW telephoned to an inspector of Special Branch and made an appointment to see him at Waterloo Station. As war had now broken out, the inspector took with him to this meeting a detention order under D.R.18B, which he served upon SNOW, who was taken into custody.

His incarceration was of short duration; after he had revealed the place of concealment of his transmitter it was brought to Wandsworth Prison, and the proposal was made that the set should be used from there to reestablish contact with Germany under our direction. The proposal was accepted and the wireless set was installed in SNOW's cell.

After some difficulty in making contact, the following message was sent: "Must meet you in Holland at once. Bring weather code. Radio town and hotel Wales ready." SNOW's explanation of this rather cryptic message was that Ritter had instructed him that one of his principal duties in time of war would be the transmission of daily weather reports, and that he was to discover the name and address of a reliable member of the Welsh Nationalist party, an organisation which the Germans proposed to use for purposes of sabotage in South Wales. There are dramatic moments in the history of most institutions, and this, in the record of double-cross activities, is one of them, for with SNOW's first message from Wandsworth Prison the double-cross system was well and truly launched. Very soon he was receiving a variety of orders and requests for information.

Later in September SNOW paid a visit to Rotterdam and there succeeded in making contact satisfactorily with Ritter. He returned from this visit with some fresh instructions and a quantity of miscellaneous information. Some weeks later he returned to the Continent, accompanied this time by G.W., a retired police inspector who had been nominated by us as SNOW's contact in the Welsh Nationalist party. Together G.W. and SNOW saw Ritter, who was this time accompanied by a man known to them as the Commander, who discussed at length with G.W. a project for shipping arms and explosives to South Wales by submarine, where they were to be used for a major insurrection by the Welsh Nationalist party. This meeting also passed off successfully, and SNOW returned with money and some fresh instructions in the shape of microphotographs reduced to about the size of a postage stamp.

One of these photographs was in the form of a letter addressed to the agent CHARLIE, with whom SNOW was instructed to put himself in contact. CHARLIE is of German origin and one of a family of three brothers. He himself acquired British nationality at birth, and has turned out to be entirely loyal. CHARLIE himself and one of his brothers were both recruited by the Germans in Cologne in 1938 and had worked for Germany, but CHARLIE had done so with great reluctance under threat of reprisals against the third brother in Germany. The object of putting SNOW in touch with him was that, being an expert photographer, he might be used by SNOW to develop the microphotographs and to reduce SNOW's own reports to the same form for easy transmission to Germany. On this same visit SNOW was informed by the Germans that he would for the future be paid by a woman resident near Bournemouth, and in fact during his absence abroad two letters arrived for him, each containing £20, which were traced to a Mrs. Mathilde Krafft, who was subsequently lodged in Holloway Prison.

So far, then, SNOW's activities had been from our point of view uniformly successful, since they had resulted in the discovery of not less than three German agents. Moreover, they had clearly indicated some of the uses to which the double agent system could be put. Some knowledge of the Abwehr personalities and methods had been gained, it was obvious that the questionnaires would give guidance with regard to enemy intentions, and in particular the embryonic sabotage plans of the Germans had been exposed sufficiently to make preparations to defeat them if they materialised.

One more gain, less obvious but perhaps even more important, dates also from these early days. This was the knowledge obtained of German wireless codes and cypher procedure. SNOW was given a code by the Germans, and the wireless operator who was in charge of his case and who was also a V.I.* undertook to monitor the transmissions from the Hamburg station, as he was able to recognise the note of the station and the style of transmitting of the various operators. As a result of this monitoring he discovered that Hamburg was working to a vessel moving up and down the Norwegian coast. The preamble and the form of the code, namely a five-letter code, which was used by our agent, turned out ultimately to be the basis of a number of codes used by the Abwehr, and the knowledge gained through the SNOW case assisted materially both in exposing the German

*Voluntary interceptor.

organisation and enabling us to break other messages transmitted by the Germans. It cannot be doubted that the SNOW case helped greatly in obtaining the early and complete mastery of the system.

In October SNOW and G.W. paid a visit together to Antwerp, where they again interviewed Ritter and the Commander. G.W. was given a little elementary instruction in methods of fire-raising and SNOW was provided with some detonators concealed in a slab of wood. G.W. was also provided with a cover address in Brussels, and it was anticipated that for the future he would communicate with the Germans to some degree independently of SNOW. Throughout the greater part of the phoney war affairs proceeded on these lines; it would be fair to say that the system continued to exist, but it did not noticeably advance or develop. SNOW continued to send wireless messages almost daily and made several visits to the Continent, but it appeared that the major sabotage plans of the Germans were postponed until the projected invasion of England should take place. On the double agent front the situation was indeed similar to that on other fronts during the phoney war—there was all the bunderbust connected with war, but very little effective action.

A lurid incident in May 1940, however, indicated that the period of waiting was nearly over and that more violent events might soon be expected. During a meeting which SNOW had with Ritter in Antwerp in April 1940, it was suggested by Ritter that a further meeting should take place between them on a trawler in the North Sea. Ritter said that he had been much impressed by the ease with which smuggling was carried on from the east coast of England, and he thought SNOW would have no difficulty in obtaining the use of a trawler for this purpose. He would himself arrive either by submarine or aircraft, and the real purpose of the meeting was to be to smuggle a new subagent, whom SNOW was to produce, into Germany, where he would undergo a thorough training in sabotage and espionage. During May this extraordinary project came to a head, and it became

necessary for us to produce upon SNOW's behalf both the
trawler and the agent. The former was produced by arrangement with the Fisheries Board and the latter was discovered
in the person of BISCUIT, an informant previously employed
by M.I.5. This man, after a prolonged career of petty lar-
ceny, dope smuggling, and the confidence trick, had re-
formed and since acted as a capable and honest informer in
criminal matters. He was accordingly introduced to SNOW,
who can have been in no doubt but that BISCUIT was acting
as an agent of this office. It is important to emphasize this
point in view of what happened later, and also because the
case of SNOW and CHARLIE had previously been run upon
the basis that neither knew that the other was controlled,
though it is clear that after a while both of them must have
guessed this fact.

On 19 May, SNOW and BISCUIT left together for Grimsby
in order to board the trawler. On the way there, unfortunately, BISCUIT formed the opinion from SNOW's behaviour and his conversation that he was acting genuinely in
the interests of the Germans and would undoubtedly reveal
his position as a controlled agent as soon as he met Major
Ritter. SNOW on the other hand appears to have been, for
reasons which we cannot analyse, under the impression that
BISCUIT was a genuine German agent who would undoubtedly reveal his, SNOW's, ambiguous position when their
meeting with Ritter took place. As a result of this he did
everything in his power to convince BISCUIT that he was
acting genuinely in the German interest, and thereby re-
doubled BISCUIT's suspicions. In this nightmare state of
mind the two boarded the trawler and proceeded towards the
rendezvous. On the evening of 21 May, which was two days
before the date fixed for the rendezvous, a plane circled
over the trawler and gave the agreed recognition signal. This
only served to convince BISCUIT of SNOW's treachery, since
both the time and their position were not what had been
previously arranged. He therefore caused the trawler lights
to be extinguished and the trawler to return home immediately, SNOW being the while kept under guard in the cabin.

On his return SNOW was searched and various documents relating to this office which he ought not to have possessed were found upon him. Further investigation revealed that these had been given him by a business associate who was short of money and had seen an opportunity of doing a profitable deal through SNOW with the Germans on the side. When he was taxed with this, the man's behaviour left no doubt of his guilt. An effort was made to retrieve the situation by despatching a trawler with a naval crew to the correct position of the rendezvous on 23 May which was the actual night fixed for the meeting. As might have been expected, however, there was no sign of any enemy aircraft or submarine. Fortunately there was a fog, and SNOW was subsequently able to represent to Ritter, apparently with success, that he had been at the rendezvous at the right time and had missed Ritter as a result of the fog.

After the North Sea episode there was, not unreasonably, some doubt as to SNOW's *bona fides*. These doubts were finally resolved in SNOW's favour, for it was clear that a great part of the trouble had had its origin in a genuine misunderstanding between SNOW and BISCUIT of each other's motives and methods of work. SNOW's case was continued as before and, since he had already told Ritter in his wireless traffic that he had recruited a new subagent in the person of BISCUIT, it became necessary, since the meeting at sea had miscarried, to arrange some other means of contact. It was therefore agreed that BISCUIT should travel to Lisbon under the cover of a dealer in Portuguese wine. He arrived in Lisbon on 27 April 1940, and there met Ritter and other German agents. To them he explained away the North Sea incident by declaring that SNOW was indeed at the rendezvous on the appointed night, but that he had seen nothing on account of the fog. Ritter confided in him that in his opinion SNOW's form was deteriorating, but that he had done excellent work in the past. He also told him that a South African was waiting in Belgium to go to England, where he would be dropped by parachute in order that he might act as an assistant or subagent to

SNOW. He asked also that arrangements should be made for the reception of sabotage material by SNOW and BISCUIT, dropped to them by parachute. The interviews and the reports handed in by BISCUIT were presumably satisfactory, for the latter returned in August bringing a further wireless set, a fresh questionnaire, and some $3,000.

The SNOW case may, therefore, be said to have been functioning normally again by the summer of 1940; at the beginning of autumn the whole state of the double agent system altered radically and developed in quite new ways.

Cautious surmise at the time, reinforced by subsequent checks at a later date, led to the conclusion that Snow was, in the early days of the war, the linchpin of the Abwehr organisation in England. It will, however, be readily appreciated that he and his assistants were not the only agents in England. Equally they were not the only double agents, and this was natural, since several different persons and organisations were playing with double agents (perhaps toying would be the better word) and attempting to secure some small, and usually temporary, advantage from them.

Most of these cases were unimportant, and the records of them are scanty, but one deserves mention because he became a permanent member of our organisation here. This was RAINBOW, who had been educated and had worked in Germany until 1938, when he returned to England. RAINBOW's espionage activities were due to his friendship with a certain "Gunther," who was sent to England under cover of representing a Hamburg chemical firm, but who actually came here for purposes of espionage. He lived in the same lodging-house as RAINBOW, and the pair were accustomed to make weekend trips into the country, when Gunther would not infrequently take photographs of factories and the like, and when he admitted to RAINBOW that he was in fact engaged in "commercial intelligence."

About a week before the outbreak of war Gunther left suddenly for Germany, but RAINBOW refrained from reporting his activities to the authorities for reasons, no doubt, of friendship as well as because of some qualms of conscience. In January 1940 RAINBOW received a letter

from Gunther in Antwerp suggesting that he should take over
the latter's agency in England. RAINBOW, interpreting this
as a proposal that he should in fact become a spy, became
with good reason nervous about his personal position and
informed the police of his association with Gunther. It was
then arranged that he should travel to Antwerp to meet
Gunther and discuss plans. The journey was duly undertaken, RAINBOW was recruited by the Germans and given
orders to report on developments in aviation and air defence,
the effect of air raids, and details of transport in the U.K. As
business cover he was given the English agency of a Belgian
firm, and instructions were to be sent to him in the shape of
microphotographs on full stops (i.e. periods) after the date
in the firm's letters to him. He was also given a good invisible
ink for his replies, a sum of money, and an address in
Antwerp through which he was to write to Gunther. In April
1940 he paid another visit to Antwerp, when he received
three more cover addresses, two in Switzerland and one in
Yugoslavia, for use in emergency. RAINBOW was therefore
well and truly started as a double agent, and later became
useful in conveying commercial and industrial information
(and misinformation) to the Germans. (The address where
he and Gunther had lived also turned out to be of some
importance as a place where the Germans believed that
assistance could be obtained for other spies in case of need.)
Gunther was later captured in Ireland and interned in
Mountjoy Prison.

Allowing for the comparative success of the SNOW network and for the potential advantages to be expected from
RAINBOW, it is still remarkable that the German efforts to
gain information from England in the first year of the war
were not more extensive. German activities in peacetime
were considerable in all countries, and it seems to be true
that the Germans trusted that enough of their peacetime
network would survive in war to supply them with the
information they needed. Incidentally, we always supposed
that the network was much larger and more effective than
it was, and many of the earlier precautions with regard to

double agents were conditioned by the belief, which turned out to be erroneous, that other and undiscovered spies were checking up on our own controlled agents. Now the Abwehr was an organisation with a particularly decentralised structure. It is true that all Stellen were controlled from Berlin, but it did not follow that different out-stations were at all informed about each other's activities. Furthermore, an individual agent was usually concerned only with one Abteilung of his Stelle,* and, if an agent of Abteilung I, was often instructed only in the work of one section of this Abteilung.

The German prewar organisation here and the organisation run during the early months of the war were almost wholly under the control of the Hamburg Stelle, and were predominantly concerned with air force matters. But in the autumn of 1940 the position abruptly and fundamentally changed. Hamburg found itself deprived of its advanced bases in neutral territories—e.g., the Low Countries and Denmark—which had been used as a starting point for new agents and as a rendezvous where established agents could report. In addition, the surviving functions of the prewar network were clearly inadequate; and, with the invasion of England looming in the future, it was necessary to seek new and better sources of information. In consequence a considerable effort was made to establish a number of agents in Great Britain in the last part of 1940. This effort, had it been made *before* the German conquest of the Low Countries, Norway, and France, might well have taxed the resources of the Security Service to the utmost; attempted when it was it led only to the establishment of a German intelligence service in Great Britain controlled by the British —in fact, to the permanent and extensive building up of the double-cross system. The reinforcements who reached this country were of different kinds—those who came through either as refugees or under business cover from neutral countries, and those dropped by parachute or landed from the sea.

*See note on p. 38.

The latter class concerns us first. In the summer of 1940 some six agents were sent to Eire, in September, October, and November over twenty-five landed in the U.K., mostly by parachute or small boat. These parachute agents played an integral part in our system, and some mention must therefore be made of the more important among them. As a rule they fell an easy prey to the Security Service, for they were imperfectly trained and equipped for their missions. Usually they had wireless sets, but in almost all cases they would have been unable to make contact without our assistance, either because of lack of technical knowledge or because of defects in the instruments themselves. An agent was generally given about £200, clearly on the assumption that he would only have to maintain himself for a month or two until the invasion took place; and his clothing, identity documents, and the like showed insufficient attention to detail and all the indications of haste and improvisation. Incidentally, the identity documents themselves were constructed on information given by the SNOW organisation, and therefore gave us clear evidence for the apprehension of newcomers.

The policy adopted was to use any of these parachute agents who could be used, since we could not tell which would be of advantage and which would not. Clearly, however, a parachutist could not be used as a double agent unless certain conditions were complied with. In the first place, his capture had to follow almost immediately on the landing—otherwise he might already have communicated with Germany; secondly, the capture had to be unobserved except by a very few, and those trustworthy, people—otherwise a statement in the press or injudicious talk would sooner or later enable the Germans to deduce that the particular spy had in fact been caught; thirdly, the spy had to be "turned round" and convinced that he could save his life by working for us; and finally, we had to satisfy ourselves that his code was understood and that messages could in fact be sent which would satisfy the Germans that the agent was actually working. These conditions were not often satisfied, and many apparently promising cases had therefore to be rejected. Some, however, satisfied our requirements and were used.

SUMMER was landed by parachute on 6 September 1940, with instructions to report on the area Oxford-Northampton-Birmingham, with particular reference to air raid damage in Birmingham itself. He was arrested within a few hours of his landing, and thereafter his story falls into two parts: what actually happened to him, and what the Germans believed to have occurred. From the German point of view SUMMER, who had injured himself slightly on landing, spent the ten days after his arrival hiding in the open between Oxford and Buckingham. Then, as the weather was bad, he proposed to find shelter for himself by posing as a refugee. The Germans vetoed this idea and instead instructed SNOW by wireless to make contact with SUMMER and arrange for his accommodation.

In 17 September 1940, SNOW despatched BISCUIT, who met SUMMER by arrangement at High Wycombe railway station. He then notionally took SUMMER with him to London, put him up in his flat and took steps to see that the seaman's papers which he had brought with him were put into order. The Germans were told via SNOW's transmitter that SUMMER had fallen ill as a result of his time in the open and was being nursed by BISCUIT. By 27 September 1940, the Germans were told that SUMMER had recovered, and that as his papers were now in order he was ready to set out once more on his own. They gave instructions that he should be told to work the area London-Colchester-Southend. By 23 October 1940 he was able to announce on his own transmitter that he had succeeded in establishing himself in lodgings to the south of Cambridge. There, as far as the Germans knew, he remained until the following January.

There was no further contact between him and SNOW's organisation except that he had BISCUIT's address for use if necessary and once received a payment of £200 from him. At the end of January 1941, SUMMER's transmitter went suddenly off the air, and the Germans were told through SNOW that BISCUIT had received a letter from him to the effect that he was under suspicion by the police and had taken advantage of his seaman's papers to cut and run. He had left his wireless set in the cloakroom at Cambridge station, whence on the Germans' instructions it was later retrieved by BISCUIT.

The true story was very different. After his capture SUMMER was accommodated at Camp 020, but later released under our control so that he might operate his transmitter. Later it was necessary to return him for a short while to Camp 020, as it had become clear from his conversation that he had not told the truth about his previous career in England. Subsequently (after a vain attempt at suicide) he was released again and installed with a guard at a house near Hinxton. Here he remained until the end of January 1941, when he made an ill-advised attempt to escape. Perhaps we had been lulled into a premature state of confidence, for he was left one day with only one guard in the house. SUMMER, though protesting that "it hurts me more than it hurts you," attacked this guard, practically strangled him, bound him, and then mounted a motor-bicycle left by one of the other guards and, with a canoe lashed to the cycle, set out for the Broads, apparently intending to attempt the sea passage to Europe. Fortunately the motorcycle, being government property, was not very efficiently maintained; it broke down, and SUMMER was apprehended at Ely after some anxious hours in which we had been compelled to warn the appropriate authorities over half England to set a watch for the fugitive.

His escape, had it succeeded, would indeed have wrecked all our schemes, but as things were no harm was done— not even to the strangled guard, who was the richer for a stimulating experience (and a good story) at the expense of some small temporary inconvenience. We, for our part, learned one lesson of primary importance which we took greatly to heart. It was this: A double agent is a tricky customer, and needs the most careful supervision, not only on the material but also on the psychological side. His every mood has to be watched, and his every reaction to succeeding events studied. For this reason we always afterwards insisted that a case officer should be personally responsible for each agent, with his hand as it were on the pulse of his patient from morning until night, and with an eye on every turn and twist of his patient's mind. In retrospect it is clear that no agent of the "converted" type could possibly survive for long unless he was studied and dealt with in this way. Without such attention he would infallibly destroy his own case in a black mood of despair or in a belated effort to restore his own self-esteem. For double agents are not as ordinary men are. As Aristotle remarked, by implication, the qualities of the good man and the good double agent are not identical in the imperfect state. Only unremitting care and some psychological finesse could coax a converted parachutist along safe lines and into a better way of thinking.

TATE, who landed by parachute in September 1940, is a shining example of the success of these principles. His arrival was not unexpected, as SUMMER had been induced to give information partly by means of a promise that the life of the friend who was to follow him should be spared. The two had been trained together and had arranged to meet in England. TATE himself eventually broke down under interrogation, was turned into a double agent, and established contact with the Germans in the middle of October. His subsequent career compared with that of SUMMER is a modern variant of the tale of the industrious compared with that of the idle apprentice. He became one of our most trusted wireless agents, and held the long-distance record as such, for he transmitted and received messages to and from Hamburg from October 1940 until within twenty-four hours of the fall of that city in May 1945.

His work was of great value, first for counterespionage purposes and later in deception,* and he was instrumental

---

*As late as the spring of 1945, TATE's messages with regard to minefields at sea were instrumental in closing an area of 3,600 square miles to German U-boats.

in securing large sums of money from the Germans. He was specially naturalised by wireless in order to receive the Iron Cross, First and Second Class, and was to end regarded by the Germans as a "pearl" among agents. Here his career was even more remarkable. So carefully was his life controlled and his secrets kept that he became to all seeming a very ordinary member of the great British public. He worked later in comparative freedom as a photographer, and was invited by one enterprising newspaper in 1944 to visit the western front and take photographs. Finally, in July 1945 it was discovered that his name had crept on to the electoral register, and that he was entitled to vote for or against the continuance of Mr. Churchill in office. Regretfully we had to dissuade him from exercising this privilege. His name will appear many times in the pages which follow; here it is only necessary to insist that his career as a double agent depended upon the successful (and difficult) handling of the case in its early days.

In the case of the parachute agents fate took a hand and often played a decisive part. GANDER, who landed on 3 October, had only a transmitting set; he was therefore only used for a few weeks until he had carried out his immediate task. JACOBS, who landed 31 January, had the misfortune to break his ankle on landing, an accident which frustrated his mission.* His arrival was widely advertised, his character was truculent, he could not be used, and he was eventually executed in August. The same fate befell Richter, who landed, in order to pay TATE, in May of 1941. He was executed in December. More interesting is the case of Ter Braak. The date of this man's arrival is unknown, but he took lodgings in Cambridge at the beginning of November 1940. His body was discovered on 1 April 1941, in a half-built air raid shelter in Cambridge, where he had committed suicide.† The rest is largely surmise, but it is more

*JACOBS carried an identity card in the name of James Rymer. Information for this name and card were sent by w/t by SNOW.
†The identity card found on Ter Braak contained five gross technical errors—a good instance of the importance of such documents for counter-espionage purposes.

than probable that he was a parachute agent (perhaps the only agent) who succeeded in eluding capture, but who was unable to make contact with the Germans. He perished when his stock of money was exhausted. It is not altogether fanciful to speculate how much more happy and more useful his career might have been if he could have fallen into the hands of the Security Service and become a double agent.

The fate of the remaining parachute agents is not germane to this history, but it is worth noting that the Security Service always opposed execution except when no other course was possible. A live spy, even if he cannot transmit messages, is always of some use as a book of reference; a dead spy is of no sort of use. But some had to perish, both to satisfy the public that the security of the country was being maintained and also to convince the Germans that the others were working properly and were not under control. It would have taxed even German credulity if *all* their agents had apparently overcome the hazards of their landing.

Descent by parachute was not the only method of entry into this country adopted by the Germans. Impressed no doubt by the prime necessity of increasing their team of active agents, they also set about introducing agents by less spectacular means. Already in September two Czechs, GIRAFFE and SPANEHL, had arrived in England. They had served in the French army and had been recruited by SWEETIE, who was working as a double-cross agent for M.I.6 in Lisbon, and who was specially employed by the Germans, and encouraged by the British, to recruit Czech agents for work in the U.K. GIRAFFE wrote a few letters and received some money, but the Germans soon complained of the paucity of the information which was sent by him, and both he and SPANEHL were allowed to serve in the French forces in the Middle East. The case was in itself of little value or importance, but it showed quite clearly that the Germans were attempting to find new ways of reinforcing their agents, and also that M.I.6 were in a position to assist materially in building up the team of double agents in this country by suitable selection in neutral countries. Further, it is now obvious that GIRAFFE's case died chiefly through lack of nourishment. Had we been in a position to furnish him with good information, or had we even had a clear policy with regard to the information which we wished to send, we might have developed him into a very useful channel. But in fact he came to us too early for us to use him properly.

Far more important was another figure who also reached us as a result of the activities of M.I.6. This was TRICYCLE, who became one of the chief figures in the double-cross world, and who became also the centre of a considerable network of other agents. TRICYCLE was a Yugoslav of good family who had been educated in France and at a university in Germany. Whilst in Germany he made the acquaintance of a certain Johann Jebsen, the son of a rich family with shipping interests in Hamburg, who afterwards became a figure of some importance in the Abwehr. In the early part of 1940 TRICYCLE's business interests brought him into relations with the German embassy at Belgrade. There one of the Secretaries insinuated that TRICYCLE, being acquainted with the wealthy Yugoslav family of Banac, had an easy *entrée* into British social circles and was therefore in a position to do useful work for Germany. Similar suggestions, perhaps only of a vague nature, were made to him by Jebsen, and TRICYCLE therefore put himself in touch with the British representative in Belgrade and asked him for advice. It was agreed that TRICYCLE should continue his conversations with the German Secretary, and eventually an arrangement was made between them by which TRICYCLE was to obtain information from England from a member (whom he did not name) of the Yugoslav legation staff in London. Questionnaires were constructed for this person, but when no answers arrived the Germans became restive and, on TRICYCLE explaining to them that his friend was afraid to use the diplomatic bag, it was finally agreed that TRICYCLE should leave for London to collect his friend's reports. Just before he left TRICYCLE had another meeting with Jebsen, who informed him that they were now both members of the same service.

On 20 December TRICYCLE, who had been acting throughout on British instructions, arrived in England. He was interrogated and created a most favorable impression. Much will have to be said hereafter about TRICYCLE and his network; for the moment it is only necessary to note that we had in him a new agent of high quality who could plausibly meet persons in any social stratum, who was well established with the Germans at the instance of an Abwehr official, and who had an excellent business cover for frequent journeys to Lisbon or to other neutral countries.

Another acquisition in the permanent working staff was DRAGONFLY, whose recruitment was of a different nature. DRAGONFLY was born in London of German parents and married a German wife. He lived in Germany from 1923 onwards and there participated in various business ventures, most of which did not prosper. On 23 August 1939 he left his flat in Cologne abruptly, abandoning his furniture, and made his home in Holland. On 29 April 1940, he returned to England. Meantime both he and his sister, a divorcee in Germany, had had certain dealings with the German Secret Service, and attempts to recover DRAGONFLY's furniture from Cologne had been instrumental in bringing him into close relations with them. He had been invited to send reports to the Germans from Holland, but had contrived not to pledge himself very far. He told the substance of his story on arrival in England, and eventually persuaded us that he could successfully make contact with the Germans again if he were sent to Lisbon. In November 1940, therefore, he departed for the ostensible purpose of conducting a deal in wine, although we had little confidence in his chances of success.

In Lisbon, however, all went well. DRAGONFLY met Kliemann, a leading figure in I Luft, Paris, received some elementary training, and returned to England in January 1941 with a wireless set disguised as a gramophone, a new cover address in Lisbon, some £800 and instructions to report on various matters, especially those connected with aircraft production and the R.A.F. He too, therefore, was well launched in his career under our control. The case differs from others in that the initiative came rather from us and from DRAGONFLY himself than from the Germans; he is almost, but not quite (having regard to his earlier and obscure dealings with the German Secret Service), a case of successful coat-trailing. The wireless communication then started continued with some intermissions and varying success until November 1943, but difficulties of securing adequate payment and the consequent rather sordid wrangles over money made his case less profitable than it would otherwise have been. To its credit, apart from the intelligence and deception importance of the transmissions, must be placed the capture of the agent JOB in November 1943.

Another method exploited by the Germans at the end of 1940 in order to obtain information was the use of well-placed neutrals in England. At a later stage some of them were able to avail themselves of the diplomatic bags of their countries. The diplomatic bag obviously represents a channel for information leaving the country which it is difficult to control and almost impossible to close down completely. But even here the double agent system was able to be of assistance, since, granted that the documents will go in any case, it is better that they should be documents dictated or suggested by us than that they should be the straightforward reports of neutral observers.

Our first contact with neutrals of the type indicated was made through G.W. (SNOW's Welsh agent) with Del Pozo, a Spanish journalist who arrived in England in September 1940. On arrival he addressed a postcard to G.W., and SNOW ascertained by wireless that he was a member of the Commander's propaganda and sabotage organisation and was in fact carrying money intended for SNOW. In October Del Pozo handed over some £4,000 in a tin of talcum powder to G.W., and the latter submitted reports on his activities in Wales. Del Pozo's actual chief was not the Commander but Alcazar de Velasco—probably he worked to

both and made a double profit. G.W.'s reports were despatched in secret writing on Del Pozo's ordinary reports,
and these were transmitted, after suitable censorship, by the
M.O.I. to Spain. At a later stage G.W.'s material was sent
by Spanish diplomatic bag.

Sufficient has now been said to make it clear that the
Germans at the end of 1940 abandoned their policy of
laissez faire and made very considerable efforts to establish
an effective organisation in this country. We for our part
adopted the policy, not of suppressing and destroying this
organisation, but rather of taking it over under our own
control—in other words, we attempted (and as the event
showed with success) to turn the German intelligence system here into a double-cross system. At this stage it is
necessary to define the objects for which the system was
run. This has been done already in the Introduction, but it
is important and can hardly be repeated too often. It is
in fact the *creed of double-cross*, and was, as it should have
been, constantly in our minds throughout the whole period
of the war. The double-cross system, then, was run for
seven specific reasons:

1. To control the enemy system, or as much of it as we
   could get our hands on
2. To catch fresh spies when they appeared
3. To gain knowledge of the personalities and methods of
   the German Secret Service
4. To obtain information about the code and cypher work
   of the German service
5. To get evidence of enemy plans and intentions from the
   questions asked by them
6. To influence enemy plans by the answers sent to the
   enemy
7. To deceive the enemy about our own plans and intentions

Dimly, very dimly, we began to guess at the beginning of
1941 that we did, in fact, control the enemy system, though
we were still obsessed by the idea that there might be a large
body of German spies over and above those whom we con-

trolled.* This idea made us somewhat timid in the early days, but did not affect the general policy. All the other objects of double cross are immensely assisted and become far more effective if and when object one is really attained. Something had already been achieved by 1941 under the headings of two, three, and four, and a little under heading five. Six and seven were still in the future, and would obviously become of major importance when British policy was able to pass from the defensive to the offensive.

*Small pieces of evidence came in early: SNOW's organisation was used to pay SUMMER, thus suggesting that it was in German eyes the safest, if not the only, source for such payments. RAINBOW's address was given as a lifeline to TATE. TRICYCLE, in order to prove his *bona fides*, told us that he had been given the name of the best and most secret of German agents here. He then produced the name and address of GIRAFFE! But of course the final confirmation of the belief that we controlled the whole came gradually from a study of secret sources.

4: ORGANISATION FOR CONTROLLING THE DOUBLE-CROSS SYSTEM

The great increase in the German organisation in this country which has been explained in the previous chapter made it essential to establish on our side an organisation capable of dealing with it. M.I.5 and M.I.6 could cope with a few cases in a hand-to-mouth manner, but clearly they could not, unaided, expect to control and run the German intelligence system in this country. Above everything else it would be necessary, if agents were to be run over a long period, to supply them with a continuous flow of traffic, and this traffic would have to be approved by responsible and highly placed persons if it was to maintain its proper level.

Not unnaturally there were institutional difficulties from the start. Even when M.I.5 and M.I.6 alone were concerned, it was not easy to secure the complete harmony and cooperation which are necessary in any jointly controlled enterprise. A newcomer, for example, might turn out to be a straight agent or a double-cross agent. It was absurd that a man outside the three-mile limit should automatically pass under the control of M.I.6, whilst within that limit he fell under the control of M.I.5. It was equally absurd that a man controlled at Lisbon by M.I.6 should pass under the control of M.I.5 at the end of his journey to this country. Again, if a campaign of misinformation was being waged, it was difficult to make sure that the efforts of straight agents and double-cross agents should be properly coordinated. In theory M.I.5 and M.I.6, for this purpose at least, ought either to have been one and the same body, or else each responsible to a common chief. Nevertheless, whilst the agents were few and whilst they were being used only for purposes of minor importance, it was possible to carry on with the improvised and rather haphazard methods of the period of the phoney war. By the end of 1940 this was no longer possible, and a proper organisation for the control and working of the double agent system had to be created.

Certain rudimentary attempts at coordination had been made already, particularly with regard to wireless agents. In July 1940 a W. Branch had been started in M.I.5, which was the origin of B.1.A.* At a higher level the W. Board was established in September 1940, and it appears from the minutes of the first meeting (30 September 1940) that the Board was set up at the instigation of D.M.I. to coordinate the dissemination of false information. In the autumn of 1940 M.I.5 and M.I.6 took steps to put the whole organisation on a proper footing, and a memorandum was sent to the Directors of Intelligence explaining to them the importance of the double agent system, telling them also that it was becoming increasingly difficult, if not impossible, to maintain the agents unless sufficient information could be released to the enemy to retain the enemy's confidence, and adding that it ought not to be impossible to strike a balance between the risks involved in releasing the minimum of true information required and the strategic losses which might result from closing the double agents down.

Fortunately D.N.I. had a keen interest in double agents and the then D. of I., Air Commodore Boyle, had himself "chanced his arm" freely in approving information for the Snow network. D. of I. took the line that knowledge of the double-cross system should be confined to M.I.5, M.I.6, and the three Directors of Intelligence,† and that risks should be taken to maintain what he felt to be potentially a weapon of great value and that the system should not be allowed to

---

*Until Sir David Petrie's reorganisation in 1941 the section dealing with double-cross agents was otherwise named, but for purposes of convenience it will be mentioned as B.I.A. throughout.

†D.M.I. changed just at this period, Major-General Davidson taking over on 16.12.40.

become a plaything of higher authorities who would not use it adequately, and would also, perhaps, boggle at the responsibilities involved. This view was generally agreed, and the W. Board, which consisted at that time of the three Directors of Intelligence, C.S.S., and the head of B. Division in M.I.5, of which B.1.A formed a part, shouldered the responsibility for maintaining the double-cross agents.*

The W. Board was on too high a level to undertake the day-to-day supervision of double agent work, and for this reason the Twenty Committee was constituted as a sub-committee of the W. Board and met first on 2 January 1941. At its first meeting the Twenty Committee included representatives from the War Office, G.H.Q. Home Forces, Home Defence Executive, Air Ministry Intelligence, N.I.D., M.I.6, Colonel Turner's Department of the Air Ministry (which was engaged in establishing dummy airfields and similar targets) and M.I.5, which provided the chairman and secretary for the Committee.†

The service interests in double agent work were sufficiently safeguarded by the three Service Directors of Intelligence. On the civil side, which turned out to be of great importance, it was necessary to obtain the same measure of support. This support was gained through the efforts of Sir Findlater Stewart, who in February 1941 arranged a meeting of the W. Board with the Lord President of the Council, Sir John Anderson, and through him the authority to provide an approving authority for all civil matters acting in the same way as the Directors of Intelligence. As a result of this meeting Sir Findlater Stewart himself joined the W. Board and became an approving authority for all traffic with which civilian departments were concerned. At the same time Lord Swinton, who was then at the head of the Home Security Defence Executive, was informed of what

---

*At a later stage Sir Findlater Stewart (H.D.E.) and Colonel Bevan (L.C.S.) were co-opted to the W. Board.
†Later Colonel Turner's representative resigned and representatives of London Controlling Station (L.C.S.) and Chief Combined Operations (C.C.O.) were added. Later still representatives from SHAEF were added.

was going on and gave the project his strong support, and later his practical assistance in the affairs of some of the agents.

For some time the W. Board exercised its responsibility fairly often in questions of policy which were referred to it. Thus it gave specific leave for SNOW to go to Lisbon in February of 1941 and for CELERY to pay a second visit to Lisbon in May of that year. In September 1941 it approved in principle of acts of sabotage being carried out without reference to it provided Sir Findlater Stewart was in agreement. In October 1941 it decided that Colonel Stanley, who then took on the control of deception, should not be informed of the work of double agents, but only that the W. Board had channels for misinforming the enemy. In December it decided that traffic was not to be approved for an agent of the Deuxième Bureau. In March 1942 it agreed that all information transmitted to the enemy should go into the pool of the Twenty Committee, which was to be regarded as the focal point for such information. These instances are given to show the function performed by the W. Board; but as time went on, being apparently satisfied that the work was being effectively done, the Board left more and more freedom to the Twenty Committee, which was in fact a meeting of those primarily interested either in the running of the agents and their traffic or in the approval of traffic, on a working level.

The Twenty Committee itself held its first meeting on 2 January 1941, and its last on 10 May 1945. It met every week and held in all 226 meetings. It thus exercised a steady and consistent supervision of all double agent work throughout the last four and a half years of the war. To it were taken all questions connected with the agents for discussion and, if necessary, decision; and its members acted as the effective approving authorities on behalf of the members of the W. Board for the traffic of agents. It discussed and carried through various plans for deceiving the enemy. It made appreciations of the questionnaires and in particular acted as a clearing-house for double agent information and as a liaison centre for the various departments concerned. At every meeting an account of the activities of the agents was given by the M.I.5 and M.I.6 representatives, so that all members of the Committee were apprised of what was going on in connection with the cases. In this way approval of information was possible without the various departments crossing each other's lines.

It cannot be denied that in many ways the organisations set up for the control of the double agent system was institutionally unsound, and questions of responsibility were never properly decided. The chairman of the Twenty Committee was instructed to summon the first meeting, but it was never made clear what his actual position was. He was appointed by the D.G.S.S. and responsible to him, but at the same time the Committee was a subcommittee of the W. Board, and the chairman of the Committee, therefore, was presumably responsible to them. Nothing in the nature of a charter or even a directive was given to the Committee. In consequence it might be held that the Committee was an offshoot of M.I.5 and M.I.6, established to obtain approval for the messages of their agents, and that the control and running of double agents remained entirely in the hands of these two departments. In the words of a note by the Security Service for the W. Board in October 1941: "The Security Service and M.I.6 remain normally the best judges as to how the machine *under their control* can be put into motion to the best advantage."

But equally it might be said (and members of the W. Board probably took this view) that the Committee was the body which controlled and ran double agents. Thus at the W. Board meeting of 11 February 1941, D.M.I. stated that "the Directors of Intelligence had taken the responsibility on their own shoulders of running the XX agents"; and in March 1942, Sir Findlater Stewart, writing to invite Sir Frank Nelson to attend a meeting connected with these problems, says: "You will no doubt be aware that a certain number of enemy agents in this country are being worked back to the enemy as *agents doubles* under control.

General direction of their activities is exercised by the W. Board. . . . Day-to-day management and control of these agents is in the hands of a joint service and civil committee (the Twenty Committee) appointed by members of the W. Board." The same view of the nature of the Committee is implicit in a circular letter of D.N.I. of 22 August 1941. In practice, however, this rather anomalous position proved no handicap. Broadly speaking, bad men make good institutions bad and good men make bad institutions good. It cannot be denied that there was some friction between M.I.5 and M.I.6 in the early days, but this disappeared when the M.I.6 representative on the Committee was changed. For the rest, the organisation had the supreme merit of working. Questions of responsibility were not raised and no one was concerned to press the interests of his own department at the expense of the general interest. In fact the control of the double agent system was an example of harmonious working between a large number of different services and different departments. In particular the services, whatever their views may have been as to the share in control which belonged to the W. Board or to the Security Service, never questioned or adversely criticised the practical control and the running of the agents by M.I.5 or M.I.6.

As the bulk of the agents concerned were those in the British Isles, it followed that the greatly preponderant share of the work fell to the lot of M.I.5 rather than to M.I.6. But here again, after the early disagreements had been overcome, complete harmony and collaboration were established between the two services. In the course of its history a vote was only once taken at the Committee, and this was due to the fact that the M.I.5 representatives were at variance with one another. All other decisions over four and a half years were arrived at after discussion without a vote. In practice, therefore, it is immaterial to discuss whether certain decisions with regard to the agents were those of M.I.5 or of the Twenty Committee, since the Committee always accepted the M.I.5 proposals, though it often offered suggestions and proposed amendments. For example, when the time came to discuss getting rid of some of the agents, an "Execution Subcommittee" was appointed by the Twenty Committee which dealt with this particular subject. What the Execution Committee in fact did was to discuss carefully with the head of B.1.A the cases of half a dozen agents suggested by him as possible victims. An agreed list was then produced, and the agents were "executed" or reprieved, as the case might be. The important point seems to be that, since everyone was working for the same ends, no one troubled to decide the academic point whether M.I.5 or M.I.6 could get rid of one or more agents without the approval of the Committee or of the W. Board.

The reorganisation was not confined to the higher levels. Within M.I.5, B.1.A. gradually developed itself into a larger section and rearranged its personnel. As has been explained above, the head of B. Division was a member of the W. Board and always maintained the keenest interest in the details and management of all double-cross cases. In consequence major decisions were always referred to him. The adoption of new agents and changes of policy were also always reported to D.G.S.S. for his approval. The section itself was controlled by a career officer of M.I.5 who was, on a working level, entirely responsible for the control of all double-cross agents in this country. As a matter of convenience he and two other officers formed an internal directorate which exercised general supervision, considered the advisability of accepting or rejecting new cases, administered the agents and their affairs, and decided questions dealing with their traffic.

Next came the case officers, who were usually about five in number. These officers dealt directly with the agents in all matters concerning their payment, housing, maintenance, guarding, and so forth. They also dealt with the preparation of the traffic and made suggestions with regard to it. In an important case the case officer practically lived the life of the agent and gave the directorate information and suggestions how the agent would in his opinion react to the questions asked of him. Next came a wireless officer, who exercised technical supervision over w/t agents and the operators employed by us for wireless purposes.* In addition, two officers were concerned with the filing and analysis of all the reports and messages sent by agents and of all questions and instructions received by them. The same officers, assisted by the case officers, were responsible for the machinery by which the information was submitted to the outside departments for approval as traffic. Another officer was responsible for the collection of all intelligence information arising out of the agents' cases. This part of the work was most important at a time when the office was collecting information about the Abwehr for purposes of comparison with the information obtained from other sources.

A bald recital of these duties gives an imperfect picture of the work done by the section, in particular with regard to the purely office side of the work. As the number of agents grew, the volume of information contained in the messages grew also to a truly formidable size, and it was highly important that all this information should be carefully indexed and readily available for reference, since the messages of any one agent at any time had to be consistent with the messages sent by him at an earlier date and (if they were to be effective) not wholly inconsistent with the messages of other agents. A single spy working on his own would be unlikely to forget what he had reported at an earlier date, but an organisation, unless great care were taken, was extremely likely to make a blunder sufficient to destroy an agent's credit. For this reason among others the work of the case officers and of the officers concerned with filing and records was of vital importance, and it was necessary for them to know the cases as intimately as though they had in

---

*This is not a technical treatise, and consequently no effort has been made to describe the work done by the wireless officer and his assistants. Any layman, however, can appreciate the fact that, though we were in wireless communication with the German S.S. for more than five years and using German procedure, our wireless experts never, so far as we can tell, made a serious mistake which could "give away" a case to the enemy.

fact lived the life of the agent themselves. Again, it must not be forgotten that a double agent does indeed live a double life. A captured agent, for example, has to live his life in this country, but at the same time has to live the life which the Germans suppose him to be living; and this second life, as reflected in his messages or letters, must be as substantial and well documented as the actual life which he is in fact leading.

In addition, the provision of suitable traffic was a day-to-day problem of pressing importance, entailing difficulties which are not perhaps apparent on a cursory survey. A newspaper reporter sent to report on a murder may well find the police anxious to allow him as little information as possible, but he will pick up something from talkative folk and he can embroider to his heart's content. A racing tout concealed under a gorse bush may get some sort of information of the favourite's form as he watches him at a practice gallop. In his case, too, he can report something to his masters. But the double agent is in a much more difficult position. First of all he has to get as best he can the answers to the questions sent to him. This meant in our cases that we would try to discover for ourselves the answers to the questions under the conditions in which a real spy would work—that is to say that our agent, or someone sent to represent him, would have to procure the information without being spotted at his task. But that is only half the story. Our agents were not a simple news agency. Once the information had been obtained, we had to put it in the form of messages and then submit it to the appropriate approving authorities.

Supposing, for example, that the agent had been asked for a report on the aerodrome at Northolt. He might collect a certain amount of information about it, but this information would then have to be approved by the Air Ministry before it could be sent over to the Germans, and it might well be that three-quarters of it would be held to be unsuitable for transmission. In other words, it would not be approved, but would be crossed out by the appropriate approving authority. Time after time, when a careful and compendious report had been got together, it was found that the greater part of it could not be approved. What was left would be sent, and the rest of the report had to be concocted to the best of our ability; and this part, too, would have to receive approval.

Only the most strenuous efforts, together with a great deal of goodwill and desire to assist on all sides, enabled us to keep up a sufficient flow of traffic to maintain and build up the cases which we desired to keep alive. Furthermore, the messages had themselves to be plausible—that is to say, they had to be of such a form and content that the Germans would readily believe them to have emanated from an honest agent. On occasion items of information which we would gladly have passed over had to be omitted or used elsewhere because they were not in harmony with the usual run of an agent's traffic. It also has to be remembered that a deception is often safer and more likely to be effective if it reaches the enemy in parts through a number of agents than if the whole of it rests upon the authority of a single agent. This meant that a good deal of careful comparison and dovetailing between the different agents had to be undertaken.

It is unnecessary to do more than indicate the sort of work and the sort of problems which B.1.A had to face. In addition, of course, the actual lives of the agents had to be regulated. That was an administrative matter which does not lend itself to description. It is probably sufficient to note that a captured and converted agent might well require a house, a housekeeper, a wireless operator, and two guards, and that his identity card, ration book, and clothing coupons would have to be procured under an elaborate cover story, since for obvious reasons we were not permitted to disclose our machinations to persons outside the organisation. Furthermore, we had to maintain special offices, disguised as business premises, where dubious characters and newcomers could be interviewed and where their conversations could, if necessary, be recorded, since we were always anxious to avoid any knowledge of our activities percolating gradually to the enemy. This same point often made the collection of traffic difficult as well, since it was not desirable or permissible to acquire information in our capacity as members of the Security Service and then transmit it to the Germans without at least hinting to the sources of that information what was being done with it.

Of necessity the running of double-cross agents entailed not only the deception of the Germans but often and in many cases the deception of people on our own side. All authorities, in particular D.M.I., were insistent from the start that the circle of those "in the know" should be as small as was humanly possible. It is quite certain that for practical purposes we informed a great many more people about some part of our work than our superiors dreamed of; but on the whole the policy of extreme secrecy was undoubtedly right and did much to keep the organisation alive and healthy up to the conclusion of the war.

The year 1941 and the early part of 1942 turned out to be a period of experiment and also a period during which the organisation was stabilised. It was a period of experiment because without very much guidance we attempted a great number of plans and pieces of minor deception, conducted partly for the purpose of deceiving and damaging the enemy, partly in order to test the agents, to try out the confidence of the Germans in them, and to examine the possibilities of using the weapon which we had to the best advantage. These experimental plans will be briefly described later. More important was the stabilisation of the organisation and the "building up" of the agents. It was always in the back of our minds that at some time in the distant future a great day would come when our agents would be used for a grand and final deception of the enemy. This glittering possibility was always the bait used when other authorities had to be persuaded to help us. It served to maintain belief in the system and was a more attractive selling point than the day-to-day counterespionage advantages which we could secure. But if the agents were ever to have their big day in the future, they had to be built up and maintained, or alternatively new agents had to be acquired to act in their place, so that at the right moment we could be sure that we had a team of trusted agents who would be ready when called upon. This building up of agents was a long and laborious process, and the basis of it was of necessity the messages which passed between them and the Germans—in other words, the traffic.

The traffic was throughout the background of all our

activities. We had so to arrange matters that it maintained its standard and its volume, that it satisfied the Germans without giving them more than was necessary and without betraying anything of real importance which could be concealed. In the traffic, in fact, what was denied to the enemy and what was suppressed was at least as important as what was conveyed to them. It is, of course, impossible to give any summary of all the questions which were asked, either in questionnaires, in supplementary questions or in personal questions to those agents who visited neutral countries, since the Germans' appetite for information was capacious, and since their questions ranged over all departments of service and civilian life.

In the period 1941 and the first part of 1942, almost all departments received attention. On the military side, questions were asked with regard to commands, corps, divisions, and brigades, including the names of commanding officers and the location of units. In order to build up their British order of battle, the Germans naturally required all the information they could get about such matters, and particularly about divisional signs and the locations of troops. At a later stage, when deception on the grand scale was practised, this particular point became of vital importance, but even as early as September of 1941 G.W. passed a document through the Spaniards to the enemy entitled: "G.H.Q., Corps and Divisional Signs," which was an early example of deception in this particular field.

The sort of question which was asked constantly can be illustrated by, for example, a question asked of DRAGONFLY in September 1942: "Have the soldiers from Weymouth themselves said they had the regimental number 153 or do they wear signs? Was Royal Tank Regiment equipped with tanks and what signs had these? What sign did the Churchill tanks have that you saw? In message 19 to 20, was the tiger's head on the red shield also worn on uniform? Where? Were they English or Canadians? Infantry or supply troops? Try to find out wherever possible the divisional numbers. Very important." Other questions which were asked concerned camps, depots and barracks, armament and equipment, and A.A. defences—e.g., to MUTT and JEFF, March 1942: "Questions regarding 4.5 A.A. guns, which interests very much. First, life of barrel in number of rounds. Second, length of barrel in calibres. Third, is the gun also manufactured in mobile form? Fourth, also details concerning use of predictor Kerason in connection with 4 cm. Bofors gun are required."

Troop movements were also of great interest, e.g., January 1941, to TATE: All information about movement of miltary units in connection with Greece and the Near East are of interest," and November 1941, TATE: "Are any parachute troops sent overseas, especially to the Middle East?" In the very early days the Germans showed great interest in defence against landings. Thus in December 1940, to SNOW: "Territory Aldington, Stowting, Lyminge, Hawkinge, Folkestone, are there any constructions or mechanisms to prevent from air landings? Said to exist on field piles connected by wire. Of which material and height are piles, which are the distances, strength of the wire?" Further questions were asked about the guage of the wire and the material of the poles, and also if connection wires were electrically charged.

Inland and coastal defences also exercised the Germans' minds. Thus TRICYCLE was asked for details of coastal defences from the Wash to Southhampton, and CELERY, in March 1941, was asked about electrically controlled land mines on the Essex, Suffolk, Yorkshire, Kent, and Sussex coasts, and also about the guns used to repel invasion. Further military questions included many on new arms, particularly antitank guns, equipment, gas, and the armament industry generally. Naval questions were on the whole less numerous than might have been expected. They concerned mainly His Majesty's ships, particularly aircraft carriers, movements of ships, later on convoys and ports, docks, and shipbuilding. Thus TRICYCLE in February 1941, was asked: "When are five battleships of King George V class ready?" and DRAGONFLY in March 1942: "Particularly interesting at

all times what you can find out about departure of convoys.
Number of ships (groups) possible time of leaving, where
assembled, where going to and protection."

R.A.F. questions on the whole predominated. They were
specially concerned with commands and locations of squad-
rons, aerodromes, R.A.F. stations, and the like. The index
of questions asked over this period shows that questions
were asked of our agents by the Germans about 288 individual aerodromes, R.A.F. stations, and bombing ranges.
A great number of questions also were asked about types
of aircraft (questions asked about some 85 individual
types), engines, armaments, parts and technical equipment,
and aircraft production also occupied a very large space.
About many of the technical R.A.F. questions FATHER,
who appears a little later in this history and who was an
expert Belgian pilot, became of especial importance, and
received embarrassingly searching questions which were
difficult to evade.

With questions such as those connected with the location
of aerodromes and factories we always had to be cautious,
lest one agent should give away another. Thus in February
1941, TRICYCLE was asked: "Do Vickers Armstrong pos-
sess factories at Brighton and Hawarden to the west of the
aerodrome? Have the buildings which were near the aerodromes and which were used for army purposes now been
taken over by Vickers for manufacturing? How many Wellingtons do Armstrong make each month? Where else are
Wellingtons or parts for Wellingtons made? We want
sketches showing sites for Vickers at Weybridge and Vickers
near Crayford." In June 1941, TATE was asked: "Adjoining
the aerodrome at Hawarden, west of Chester, there is at
the south-west corner 1km. north of village of Broughton,
the Vickers factory on the surface. Where is the underground factory? Are the works in operation?"

Questions which we roughly classed under Home Defence because the answers were approved by H.D.E. included questions on agriculture, food and exports and
imports, rationing, identity documents, air raid damage,

details of the evacuation of towns, and morale, together
with a great number concerning factories and industry
generally. In the period up to the autumn of 1942 questions
were asked about 354 individual factories and firms.*

It will be appreciated that in 1941 we were operating
agents who communicated by all three methods—i.e., by
wireless, by secret writing, and by personal contact in
neutral countries—and that the questionnaires and supplementary questions had begun to give a fairly comprehensive
picture of the German objectives. By the end of the year
we had, or had had, under our control agents operated from
Oslo, the Iberian Peninsula, Hamburg, Brussels, Brest,
Paris, and Berlin, and it was found that a kind of pattern
was developing, since each Stelle had its special character-
istics and tasks. Different agents from the same Stelle always
bore a certain family resemblance to each other. Oslo (or
the Bergenstelle which was under Oslo's control) was interested in weather conditions, but only in the north. Its agents
in England were not as a rule concerned with weather
reports, and it showed also a lack of interest in service
matters. The things which chiefly concerned it were general
conditions in this country, counterespionage, and sabotage.

*Some idea is given of the range of these questions by an extract from the
index under B: Babcock & Wilcox, Ltd., Borehamwood; Bailey, Sir W. H.,
& Co. Ltd., Manchester; Belfast Power Station; Belling & Lee, Ltd., Bore-
hamwood; Bender, F., & Co. Ltd., Borehamwood; D. G. Bennington & Co.
Ltd., Hull; Bird (Sidney) S. & Sons, Borehamwood; Birmingham Battery
Metal Corporation; Blackburn Aircraft Ltd., Brough; Bodey, Jerrim &
Denning, Bristol; Boulton Paul Aircraft Ltd., Bilbrook, Norwich, and
Wolverhampton; Bovis Ltd., Cricklewood; Bowden (Engineers) Ltd.,
Hayes; Bradford (Thos.) & Co. Ltd., Manchester; Bradshaw Brothers Ltd.,
Leicester; Brick Works, Llandudno; Bristol Aeroplane Co. Ltd., Filton,
Glasgow, and Weston-super-Mare; Britannia Iron and Steel Works Ltd.,
Bedford; British Bellanca Aircraft Ltd., Speke and Liverpool; British
Manufacture and Research Co. Ltd., Grantham; British Oxygen Co. Ltd.,
Bristol, Manchester, and Cardiff; British Power Boat Co. Ltd., Hythe;
British Ropes Ltd., London; British Thomson-Houston Co., Ltd., Coven-
try; Brockworth Aircraft Works, Gloucester; Broughton Copper Co. Ltd.,
Brooklands Works, Weybridge; Brown (John) & Co. Ltd.; B.S.A. Co. Ltd.,
Coventry and Small Heath, Birmingham; Burroughs & Welcome Ltd.,
Dartford.

The agents from the two peninsular Stellen, Lisbon and Madrid, required information on service matters, the flow of armaments and raw materials from America, food supplies and public morale, and shipping intelligence. Hamburg, which was originally charged almost exclusively with the affairs of this country, naturally asked many questions of a domestic nature and questions concerned with the daily life and interests of the agents themselves. It also insisted whenever possible on daily weather reports, and for the rest its questions were predominantly those of the air force. Another distinguishing mark of Hamburg agents was that they were nearly always given specific geographical areas in which to work. Brussels turned its attention in the early days largely to the Dungeness peninsula, with the subsidiary objectives of the Military Canal and the Dover–Canterbury railway, and it also showed interest in the east coast. Brest was especially concerned with sabotage, and Paris asked for general information and weather reports. Agents controlled directly from Berlin received those sorts of questions which would be expected to come from headquarters rather than from an outlying Stelle—i.e., questions on political and organisational matters.

The most interesting point with regard to the traffic up to the beginning of 1942 is the evidence which it gives of enemy intentions (point five of the "creed" mentioned on page 58, to which once more reference should be made). In retrospect it is perfectly clear, even if it was not quite clear at the time, that enemy intentions could be gauged from the traffic of our agents with very fair accuracy. In R.A.F. matters, for example, the majority of questions with regard to aerodromes was concerned all through the Battle of Britain with the position and defences of *fighter* aerodromes. Conversely, in 1941, when the British air offensive on the Continent started, interest swung over to *bomber* aerodromes and the landing grounds from which bombers operated. The extent of the danger to this country of invasion from Germany is naturally clearly mirrored in the messages. In the autumn of 1940 questions are sent about defences in this country, especially in the southeast and east of England—in other words, invasion was contemplated, and our answers were naturally framed to avert this by exaggerating the strength of the defences wherever possible.

The change in enemy intentions is made especially obvious by a study of the questions with regard to foodstuffs. There were a number of these in the autumn of 1940, which were apparently in connection with invasion plans, since apart from the questions about the location of depots, G.W. was asked to try to arrange sabotage for factories and warehouses where commodities were manufactured and stored. In the spring of 1941, when it became evident that the war might be long, questions with regard to food began to take a different form. They dealt less with the location of stores and more with the food situation in the country; and details were demanded of the rations of meat, butter, fat, eggs, etc., for the civilian population. Further enquiries were made whether amounts shown on the ration cards were actually obtainable. In the summer the same tendency was observable; demands were made that details should be sent of the actual amounts of food arriving in this country from Canada, the United States, and South America. Prices of foodstuffs were also demanded.

By and large, the obvious deduction from the spring and summer food questions was that the Germans had turned away from the theory of the quick decision and were placing more reliance upon the long-distance effects of the blockade. The influence on morale of food shortage and rising prices would be extremely important among the lower classes of society, and this fact probably explains the use made by the enemy of THE SNARK, who, as a domestic servant, could not be expected to be of any value except as a reporter on such topics as retail prices and complaints of minor practical inconveniences. In August 1941 a memorandum was written and sent to Home Forces, pointing out these facts and adding that the insistence of the Germans on the personal security of their agents (some of whom had been

instructed to lie low and take no risks) led us to the conclusion that the Germans had abandoned, at any rate for
1941, the idea of any large-scale offensive operations
against this country, and were concerned to preserve their
agents for the following year. This view confirmed appreciations of the situation built on other evidence which had
already been made by Home Forces.

In the autumn of 1941 and the early winter of 1941-42
both types of food question were asked. TATE received elaborate questions about retail prices and stocks of commodities in August, and in September was asked to investigate
the "many underground food stores" in England. RAINBOW
was asked about the location of food dumps, especially
about the "large stocks" in Oxford. THE SNARK, on the other
hand, was asked for further details of prices and of the
difficulties of the purchaser. SWEET WILLIAM was charged
to report comprehensively on the food situation and on
anything which had a bearing on the effects of food shortage
on the army, the government, and the general public. Finally, BALLOON in December received several communications concerned with food supplies, food storage, and
deliveries from the United States.

In attempting to appreciate this information we were
able to discard the old explanation that locations of food
dumps were required for purposes either of bombing or of
sabotage. That policy had never been successful, and it is
obvious that food dumps are singularly ill-fitted as objects
of attack by either of these two methods. The invasion angle,
however, could not be left wholly out of consideration, since
an invading force would certainly consider knowledge of
the localities in which food in large quantities could be procured as a piece of vital information; or alternatively, it
might wish to deny us the benefits of these localities by the
use of persistent gas. Conceivably, then, the questions might
have indicated a renewed invasion project for the spring of
1942. On the whole, however, we came to the clear conclusion that the questions heralded not invasion but an
intensification of the blockade, and this was the deduction

made by BALLOON, who, of course, could judge only from his own traffic and without the assistance of the information coming from other agents. Furthermore, Lord Woolton's statement of 11 January 1942 to the effect that ships would have to be taken off convoy work in order to take reinforcements and supplies to distant theatres of war would no doubt tend to encourage German efforts to intensify the blockade and to reduce British morale by bringing about a shortage of commodities. To this there was a highly satisfactory side: the anxiety of the Germans to discover details about the destination of British troops going overseas, together with their keen interest in the training and strength of parachute troops, seemed to show us a shifting from an offensive to a defensive attitude of mind on the part of our enemies.

This perhaps overelaborate examination of questions on foodstuffs is only an example of the sort of information which the traffic could give with regard to enemy intentions. Another startling example is to be found in TRICYCLE's questionnaire for America, which contained a sombre but unregarded warning of the subsequent attack upon Pearl Harbour. TRICYCLE had established himself as a leading and highly placed agent in England and had made two more visits to Lisbon, the first in January and the second in March and April, 1941. So much was he trusted that it was arranged that he should go to America (at the behest of the Germans) in order to start a large-scale espionage network for them there. He accordingly left England on 26 June, stayed for some time *en route* in Lisbon, and finally departed for America on 10 August, carrying with him his questionnaire concealed under a series of full stops. On 19 August we received copies of the questionnaire from M.I.6, and this questionnaire was read to the Twenty Committee and translations were sent to service members. It will be remembered that the full stops were photographed and enlarged by the F.B.I. in America, who were therefore in possession of all the information contained in the questionnaire. The questionnaire itself formed the instructions for TRICYCLE, who was being sent over by the Germans to America with a view to establishing an important information organisation there—important particularly because the greater part of their previous organisation had been discovered and broken up.

The whole questionnaire covers approximately three quarto sheets typed, and of this one-third deals with Hawaii and in particular with Pearl Harbour. It is noticeable that, whereas all the other questions are more or less general or statistical (e.g., "Reports regarding U.S.A. strong points of all descriptions, especially in Florida"; "How much is the monthly production of bombers, fighting planes, training planes, civilian aeroplanes?"), those connected with Hawaii are specialised and detailed (e.g., details of named aerodromes, if possible with sketches, and the situations of the hangars, workshops, bomb depots, and petrol depots are demanded). Another characteristic question is: "Pearl Harbour—exact details and sketch of the situation of the State Wharf and the power installations, workshops, petrol installations, situation of Dry Dock No. 1 and the new dry dock which is being built."

TRICYCLE was to operate in the United States generally and would presumably be for some length of time in the eastern states. It is therefore surely a fair deduction that the questionnaire indicated very clearly that in the event of the United States being at war, Pearl Harbour would be the first point to be attacked, and that plans for this attack had reached an advanced state by August 1941. Obviously it was for the Americans to make their appreciation and to draw their deductions from the questionnaire rather than for us to do so. Nonetheless, with our fuller knowledge of the case and of the man, we ought to have stressed its importance more than we did. With the greater experience of a few more years' work, we should certainly have risked a snub and pointed out to our friends in the United States what the significance of the document might be; but in 1941 we were still a little chary of expressing opinions and a little mistrustful of our own judgment. The lesson is, no doubt, that once an agent is firmly established, any questionnaire given to him has a much greater and more immediate intelligence value than that usually attributed to it. TRICYCLE's questionnaire for America is given in full in Appendix 2.

6: EXPERIMENTAL PLANS IN 1941

Apart from the traffic, the chief interest of 1941 lay in the experimental plans and deceptions carried out or attempted at that time. These exercised the ingenuity of the members of B.1.A and of the Twenty Committee, and some of them showed a dividend, but a very great number failed or turned out to be impracticable. No exaggerated regrets need be wasted on those that failed, for the reason for failure was almost always the same. It was this: there was no coordinated or energetic direction of large-scale deception, and consequently only those plans could succeed which we were in a position to carry out among ourselves and without detailed directives. Had we been told, for example, that it was desirable to convince the Germans that we were about to invade Denmark or to attack Dakar, we could probably have contrived to carry out the task, provided that adequate support was given by troop movements, service wireless messages and the like. But we seldom knew authoritatively what was desirable and what was not.

On the other hand, any project which we could effectively control ourselves and carry through with the assistance of the Service members of the Twenty Committee usually flourished. Some of the 1941 plans must receive a brief mention here in order to illustrate the type of work which was being done.

PLAN I. This was inaugurated at the second meeting of the Twenty Committee, and consisted in the construction of a dummy ammunition dump, which was made in order that the Germans might be enticed to bomb it. The dump was ready in March and the requisite messages were sent by

TATE, but there was no result and the dump had to be dismantled.

PLAN STIFF. This plan was to drop by parachute in Germany a wireless set, instructions and codes, and to persuade the Germans that an agent had been dropped but had abandoned his task. It was hoped both that the Germans would have to undertake a search for the missing agent and also that they would "play back" the set to us, which would enable us to learn a great deal about their technique of deception. Practical difficulties prevented this plan, though it was revived on many occasions, from being executed.

PLAN MACHIAVELLI. This plan required the transmission through TRICYCLE of certain fictitious charts of east coast minefields. Some of the documents reached the Germans, but did not arouse their interest or establish their confidence to the extent which we had hoped.

PLAN IV. This was the first of a number of successful attempts to pass false documents to the enemy. We had received a directive from the Air Ministry that we were to attempt to draw away aerial attack from towns and factories and to attract it to aerodromes. It was realised that the enemy would drop their bombs somewhere, and it was regarded as greatly preferable that they should bomb aerodromes where they could be properly received, rather than towns which were very imperfectly defended. In consequence a number of documents were constructed and placed in a folder which was supposed to have been stolen by a messenger in one of the ministries. The documents included papers for a meeting of the Air Raid Review Committee and reports on damage caused by German air attacks at the end of February and the beginning of March. The various papers indicated alarm amongst those concerned at the effect of any attacks which had been made on aerodromes, and stressed the imperfections of the defence there and the weakness of the training. They also suggested that a great number of British aeroplanes had been destroyed on the ground.

The folder, after other attempts had failed, was successfully conveyed by G.W. through the Spanish embassy. The exact effect of the plan was impossible to gauge, but in 1945, when German Air Ministry files fell into British hands, it was discovered that the plan had apparently had very considerable success. The Germans accepted the documents at their face value* and drew the conclusion which was desired, that attacks on aerodromes would be the most effective use of the Luftwaffe. The first conclusion which the German commentator makes reads in translation as follows: "The British ground organisation concentrated in the southeast of England is the Achilles heel of the R.A.F. A planned attack on the ground organisation will hit the British air force at its most tender spot."

PLAN PEPPER. This was a plan to discredit the German Consul-General in Barcelona on the basis of information given by CELERY. The necessary messages were sent by DRAGONFLY but their effect remained doubtful. At a later date a much more elaborate plan, PLAN PAPRIKA, was

---

*German Air Ministry File I/C.III.V.D.

Ic/III A   II.Qu., den 20.8.1941.

VORTRAGSNOTIZ

Betr.: Angriffe auf die brit. Bodenorganisation.

Durch die Abwehr wurde 1 Hefter brit. Originalakten beschafft, weicher die Sitzungsunterlagen des Mr. J. A. Drew (Home Defense Executive= Kommandeur [m.s note "Beauftragter" or "Zivil Bevollmächtigter"] der Heimat-Verteidigung) [Ziv. Luftschutz.] für die wöchentliche Sitzung des Air Raid Review Committee=Berichtsausschuss, für Luftangriffe auf England (vom 5.3.41) enthalt. Die Unterlagen umfassen neben einigen Briefen das Protokoll der letzten Wochensitzung (28.2.41) sowie die halbtäglichen und den wöchentlichen Bericht über die durch deutsche Luftangriffe augerichteten Schäden in der Zeit vom 26.2.-5.3.41 (Home Security Intelligence Summary=Ubersichtsbericht Lage England bzw. Home Security Weekly Appreciation=Wöchentliche Gesamtbeurteilung Lage England). Das Sitzungsprotokoll ist abgesehen von seinem sachlichen Inhalt interessant wegen der typisch englischen "vereinsmässigen" Behandlung militarischer Fragen. Eine Auswertung der genannten Unterlagen (26.2.-5.3.) durch Gegenüberstellung der brit. Berichte und der dentschen Angriffsmeldungen (Lagebericht) ist in Arbeit.

evolved in order to cause friction in the German hierarchy in Belgium. A long series of wireless messages was constructed containing sufficient indications in code names and the like to allow the Germans to guess which of these high officials were engaged in a plot to make contact with certain British persons with a view to peace negotiations. This plan had to be abandoned because P.W.E. were unable to decide what they wished to have done. As on other occasions, our system was not exploited as fully as it might have been on the political side.

PLAN MIDAS. This was a successful financial plan—successful no doubt because we were able to carry it through without reference to other departments. In Lisbon TRICYCLE represented to the Germans that he knew a rich Jewish theatrical agent who was anxious to build up a reserve of dollars in America as he was afraid England might lose the war. The arrangement made, therefore, was that TRICYCLE should receive dollars in Lisbon or America from the Germans and that the Jew should pay over £20,000 in sterling to TRICYCLE's nominee in England. The nominee was, of course, to be a person chosen by the Germans. The Germans clutched with avidity at this offer and sent a financial expert to Lisbon to consider the project and to work out details. As a result the dollars were paid by the Germans to TRICYCLE, less a not inconsiderable rake-off which apparently went into the pockets of Abwehr officials, and the Germans instructed TATE to collect the sterling from the Jew in London. All this was carried out and the money was notionally handed over to TATE, who reported its safe receipt to the Germans.

The value of the operation to us was considerable. Our agents were built up in the confidence of the Germans; TATE was, in German eyes, put in control of a very large sum of money which would enable him to pay other agents or undertake more costly commitments; we secured a considerable sum of money and were confirmed in our belief that we controlled the effective part of the German organi-

sation in this country. In addition, those members of Kriegs-
organisation (K.O.) Portugal who had to deal with TRI-
CYCLE saw that they had in him an agent through whom
they could secure advantages, both material and in prestige,
for themselves, and they were always concerned to bolster
up the TRICYCLE case if and when any suspicion of it
arose in Berlin.*

PLAN OMNIBUS. This plan was an attempt made at the
request of the War Office to create the threat of an invasion
of Norway. The agents used were DRAGONFLY, BALLOON,
GELATINE, and MUTT and JEFF—the last-named pair doing
the bulk of the work. A threat was created by a number of
unrelated reports all suggesting that a force was being created and trained to invade Norway. These messages were
sent concerning refugees from Norway, special training of
troops in Scotland, advertisements for fishermen with
knowledge of the coast of Norway, inspections by the King
of Norway in Scotland, and personal suggestive remarks by
officers who were supposed to be about to embark on some
new enterprise.

The details are unimportant, but it seems that the Germans took the threat seriously, for they promised a special
bonus of £500 to MUTT and JEFF for more exact information concerning British landing intentions. The plan was
allowed to drop in September and could not have been fully
effective since it was not sufficiently supported by corrob-
orative evidence or movements of troops. It indicated,
however, once more, how much might be done if an energetic and powerful deception executive could come into
being.

PLAN MICAWBER. This plan was designed to introduce to
the Germans a new agent working in Censorship. In other
words, it was a coat-trailing attempt which failed since the

---

*Information secured after the end of hostilities supports our surmise that
some Abwehr officials wilfully shut their eyes to suspicions about these
agents. They thought it better for selfish reasons to have corrupt or dis-
loyal agents than to have no agents at all. This point is well brought out in
the report on Major Friedrich Busch.

Germans did not pursue the matter. On the other hand, it should not be forgotten that the essence of counterespionage is prevention, and the failure of this plan helped to satisfy us that the Germans were not in fact making any real attempt to use censorship leakages for their own purpose. Very often we have to remind ourselves that the most real successes of M.I.5 are represented by the fact that certain things never happened at all. Censorship, which in the last war was a favourite field for attempted espionage work, seems in this war to have been extremely effective, and was not seriously assailed by the Germans at all.

PLAN GUY FAWKES. A similar judgment is broadly true with regard to sabotage. At the beginning of the war we were, with reason, afraid that a great campaign of sabotage would be carried out by the enemy in this country. In truth and in fact very little sabotage was done or even attempted, but in the early days it was thought, and rightly thought, that the most important work of our double-cross agents might well be on the sabotage side, that is to say, they might help us to arrest other saboteurs resident in or sent to this island. G.W. was primarily a sabotage agent. His earliest tasks were to raise recruits among the Welsh Nationalist party for sabotage in Wales, and he also discussed the possibility of the poisoning of water supplies. G.W. himself in his dealings with the Germans always sniffed at the task of collecting intelligence reports which was demanded of him, and proudly pointed out that he was by profession an expert in sabotage and that he felt it something of a slur on his reputation that he should be employed in what he considered a less honourable sphere of activity.

MUTT and JEFF were also primarily sabotage agents and it was not easy to coax the Germans into the belief that the more important part of their work was that of sending information. It therefore seemed necessary to allow them to carry out a piece of sabotage in order to reestablish their reputation with their German masters, to secure payment for them, to get information about other sabotage projects of the enemy and, most important of all, to secure specimens of the most up to date German sabotage equipment. The W. Board gave approval in principle to the use of double agents for acts of sabotage and in consequence PLAN GUY FAWKES was carried out in November 1941. It consisted in arranging a minor explosion in a food dump at Wealdstone. Put in this bald fashion the operation sounds simple and uninteresting. In fact double-cross sabotage, of which this was the first example in this war, is highly complicated and excessively difficult to conduct successfully. It must be remembered that to get full value on the German side lurid accounts of the explosion have to appear in the press, but the press very properly will only put in accounts which their reporters can send to them. In other words the press has to be deceived by us as well as the Germans, and if the explosion or wreckage has not been considerable, the reports in the press will, if they appear at all, be correspondingly meagre.

In this particular case a high official at the Ministry of Food had to be taken into our confidence, as well as the Commissioner of Police at Scotland Yard, but even so there were many ticklish moments before the operation was successfully completed. The two aged fire guards at the food store could only with difficulty be roused from slumber and lured away from that part of the premises where the incendiary bomb had been placed. A too zealous local policeman almost succeeded in arresting our officers, and it was a matter of great difficulty to ensure that the fire resulting from the explosion should be sufficiently fierce to cause excitement in the district and yet not great enough to cause serious damage before the fire brigades could overcome it. The subsequent history of double-cross sabotage will occur later in this record. Here it is only necessary to say that this first essay did in fact secure some at least of its objects.

Minor pieces of deception which could not attain the dignity of being classed as "plans" were carried out throughout the period to assist the various services. These consisted for the most part in passing across misinformation to the enemy, for example in technical matters or production and on our own defences. At a later stage, as will be seen in chapters 11 and 12, these matters took on a vastly greater importance and had highly satisfactory results; in 1941 we were only trying out and testing our weapons.

The discussion of the traffic and of the plans of 1941 has gone ahead of the history of the system itself and of the agents, to which we must now return. Running a team of double agents is very like running a club cricket side. Older players lose their form and are gradually replaced by new-comers. Well-established veterans unaccountably fail to make runs, whereas youngsters whose style at first appears crude and untutored for some unexplained reason make large scores. It is not always easy to pick the best side to put into the field for any particular match. With our double agents the object was always to have a thoroughly well-trained and trustworthy team, changing the personnel to the best advantage and ready always to take the field for what might be a decisive match. In addition some of the players required a good deal of net practice before they were really fit to play in a match. The prime difficulty was that we never knew the date when this decisive match would take place, and our best batsmen and the ones we had most carefully trained might be past their best or even deceased before the date of the final game.

The first big change in the team came early in 1941 with the collapse of SNOW (who had always till then batted at number one) and his assistants. In January it was arranged that SNOW should go to Lisbon to meet Dr. Rantzau and that he should take CELERY with him. CELERY himself was a new acquisition. He had served in a branch of Air Intelligence in the last war, but in the second war he had failed to regain a commission in the R.A.F., in circumstances which enabled him to represent himself to the Germans as having a grudge against this country. An enterprising and observant man, he had marked down SNOW and had indeed trailed both him and the head of B.1.A. on his own initiative, believing that he was on the track of real German spies in this country.

The obvious policy was to turn the poacher into a gamekeeper: he became a nominee of this office and SNOW arranged to take him with him to Lisbon, picturesquely describing him to Rantzau as one of his new "side-kicks." They were to receive some training from the Germans and to return here to continue their work. Our own objects in sending CELERY to Lisbon were that he should (a) clarify and report on SNOW's position abroad; (b) observe and report on the German espionage system in Portugal; and (c) enter Germany, if the Germans would take him, and there penetrate the German Service and bring back what information he could.

What exactly happened on the visit of SNOW and CELERY is still to some extent a matter for speculation. SNOW travelled by air and arrived first; CELERY followed by sea. According to SNOW's account he was bluntly accused by Rantzau of having double-crossed him and on his own admission gave away all the secrets of his wireless transmissions and his dealings with us. According to CELERY's account, when he arrived no mention was made by SNOW to him of this disaster, and he was, after various preliminaries, conveyed to Germany, where he spent some three weeks, mainly at Hamburg. There he was subjected to a devastatingly thorough interrogation, which he survived, and he was taken for a personally conducted tour over the city. SNOW, overcome by illness, alcohol, and jealousy, remained in Lisbon. Both returned together to this country, carrying with them some new sabotage material, including fountain pens fitted with detonators, and £10,000.

An exhaustive enquiry was made into this extraordinary story, since the facts appeared to contradict one another to an astonishing extent. If indeed SNOW had revealed all, why was CELERY not painfully executed by the Germans in Germany, unless perchance he had gone over to the enemy?

If, again, all had been revealed, why did the Germans present SNOW with £10,000? If SNOW was really, to use his own phrase, "rumbled," why did he not warn CELERY of the immense danger of entering Germany? He said that he did, but CELERY maintained that he knew nothing of all this till we informed him in London. The riddle of the Sphinx and the doctrine of the Trinity are simple and straightforward affairs compared with this double enquiry. On the whole the most likely hypothesis, among the many that we formed to account for these strange happenings, was that SNOW had not in fact been "rumbled" at all, but had invented this part of the story because the complications of his position were getting too much for him. A long incarceration, however, never brought him to change his story.

Whatever the truth might be, it seemed right to give the Germans the minimum of exact information and a series of messages was therefore sent by SNOW's transmitter saying that the chief was extremely ill; that his nerve and health had collapsed, and finally, that it was impossible to carry on and that the gear would be packed up and hidden. The SNOW case thus came to an end, and with it also the cases of CELERY, BISCUIT, and CHARLIE, though CELERY was sent on another but abortive visit to Lisbon. He subsequently entered the business world, and disappeared from our ken.

The consequences of this breakdown were not quite so serious as had at first been anticipated. G.W., who had originally been a SNOW agent, had established himself on his own. He had got into touch with the Spaniard, Del Pozo, and had discussed with him the working of sabotage in Wales. In January Del Pozo had actually suggested that when sufficient money arrived the two should buy a car and go a-sabotaging together. G.W. himself, as was mentioned above, always complained to the Germans that his abilities as a saboteur were underrated. The partnership, however, was broken up when Del Pozo left England in February. It was not until June that G.W. got into touch with the Spaniards again through a porter at the Spanish embassy. He then worked himself into the confidence of Calvo, who was press attaché there. This partnership for a time proved brilliantly successful, for G.W. was able to pass over documents of the highest importance for us through the Spanish diplomatic bag. These included the divisional signs document, the air raid damage report, and information about the Malta convoy. In fact, G.W. became our best channel for the transmission of documents and information too bulky or detailed for transmission by wireless.

The rest of the old gang continued to operate. TATE, whose situation, from the German point of view, was that of a free agent with no regular employment, was chiefly concerned with a series of attempts to secure adequate payment. He had not been amply provided for when he arrived because the Germans optimistically supposed that they would soon follow him to England. As his money dwindled he was compelled to plead for assistance, and a series of attempts was made to help him. He secured £100 by registered post through SNOW and entered into negotiations to receive money through RAINBOW, or in an emergency from an aeroplane which was to drop £500 for him. The Germans abandoned this last idea when they were able to tell him that a friend from Hamburg would personally bring over the money and a new crystal for him.

A complicated series of meetings was arranged at the Regent Palace Hotel, the Tate Gallery, and the British Museum, but the rendezvous was never kept although the imminent arrival of a second friend was announced to him. In fact Richter, who had been one of the friends, was arrested and subsequently executed. He could hardly be blamed, therefore, for failing to attend the meeting. Finally the Germans instructed TATE to wait at 16.00 hours at the terminus of the Number 11 bus route at Victoria. He was there to enter a bus with a Japanese who would be carrying *The Times* and a book in his left hand. TATE was to wear a red tie and also to carry a newspaper and a book. After the fifth stop they would both alight and continue their journey by the next bus on the same route where, after an exchange of agreed remarks, the Japanese would hand the paper over to him. In it money would be found. TATE replied to this message by pointing out that the Number 11 bus no longer had its terminus at Victoria, and proposing Number 16 instead, and eventually after further delays and difficulties the operation was actually and successfully performed. Special Branch watched the whole affair, photographs were taken, and the Japanese, who rather naively returned directly to his embassy, was identified as one of the assistant naval attachés, Lieut. Commander Mitinory Yosii. TATE, by this method, received £200.

In actual fact the incident was unimportant, but it does not need much imagination to realise that had circumstances fallen out otherwise this evidence of the espionage activities of a then neutral power might have been of considerable value. In July TATE received (as the Germans thought) £20,000 as the result of the operation of Plan MIDAS, which has been described above. The difficulties of securing the early payments for TATE were not without their value for the case. A real agent would, in fact, have had grave difficulties to overcome, and the tiresome hitches and obstacles can only have served to confirm the Germans in their belief in the case.

Once the MIDAS money had been paid we realised that TATE's position was really too good. With so much money he would be able to move about too freely and to see too much and would therefore be unable to declare his inability to secure the answers to awkward or embarrassing questions. Consequently in September he informed the Germans that he had been questioned by the police about his failure to register for military service, but that he got out of his difficulties by explaining that a friend of his, whose daughter he had at one time been able to help, had certified that TATE had been doing indispensable work in his firm and had now been offered a position as right-hand man on his farm—a position which would secure him exemption from military service. The benefit derived from this state of affairs was that TATE could not leave the farm except occasionally at weekends, and was therefore unable to take long journeys, unless we specially wished him to do so. This met the difficulty raised by the Germans' suggestion that as a rich man he should move in a better social circle and get into touch with more important people. We did arrange, with an eye to the future, that he should meet a friend of his employer's daughter (who visited the farm at weekends) and who turned out to be a girl engaged in the cypher department of one of the ministries. She was later lent by her ministry to the Americans and turned out to be a very useful source of information. It should perhaps be added that during a period when he was ill, TATE's trans-missions had been operated by one of our own men who had learned to imitate his style, and thenceforward though TATE assisted in the drafting of his messages he was not permitted actually to operate himself.

DRAGONFLY's case proceeded normally. He was supposed by the Germans to have secured a position in his local food office, but his traffic, apart from a long-drawn-out battle over payments, was chiefly important for the daily weather reports which he sent. RAINBOW developed into a more important agent than we had a right to expect. His real and supposed position was that he was employed in Weston-super-Mare as pianist in a dance band, but the Germans agreed at the end of the year to pay him a salary of £1,000 a year so that he could transfer his activities to London. In February 1942 he obtained work in a factory, and his traffic became more and more concerned with industrial and economic topics.

TRICYCLE meantime had prospered. Suitable answers were provided to his questionnaires, and in January he returned to Lisbon, where he had a series of successful interviews with Von Karsthoff. They discussed plans for the future, and it was agreed that if suitable cover could be arranged TRICYCLE should go to America, if he could appoint some reliable person to carry on his work in England. He returned in February to this country and recruited two subagents—

BALLOON, an ex-army officer, at that time secretary to a firm dealing in small arms, who had previously had to resign his commission after finding himself in financial difficulties; and GELATINE, a woman of Austrian origin, who had previously worked as an agent for M.I.5 and who had good contacts in political circles. The idea was that these two subagents should be unknown to each other, and that BALLOON should answer the technical and military questions proposed by the Germans, whilst GELATINE dealt exclusively with the political side.

TRICYCLE visited Lisbon again in March, taking with him answers to his questionnaire and a chart of east coast minefields which he was supposed to have obtained from a naval officer. The arrangements made with regard to BALLOON and GELATINE were approved, but the chart was considered to be out of date and was not appreciated as highly as we had hoped. TRICYCLE returned to England for the purpose of making final arrangements with BALLOON and GELATINE; but he left again in June, arranged Plan MIDAS on his passage through Lisbon, and departed for America. Of his subagents, BALLOON prospered at once and was able to fill TRICYCLE's place in this country; but GELATINE's letters, probably because they were concerned with political matters, excited very little interest.

Meantime new agents had joined us. MUTT and JEFF arrived in this country on 7 April 1941, having been put into a boat near the south shore of the Moray Firth from a German seaplane which had flown from Norway. They immediately gave themselves up to the authorities. They had a two-way w/t set, a sum of money, forged and out-of-date travellers' ration books, detonators, and bicycles. MUTT was the son of a Norwegian father and a British mother and had British nationality through having been born in London. He spoke English, German, and Norwegian fluently. JEFF was also a Norwegian and a fluent linguist.

The primary mission for the two was to sabotage food dumps and other objectives in Scotland, for which purpose they were equipped with recipes for incendiary bombs and rough particulars of objectives. Their secondary mission was to report by wireless upon air raid damage, troop movements, and civilian morale. MUTT, whose *bona fides* was established, was after a time allowed to live at liberty in London operating his transmitter under our control, whilst JEFF, whose temperament was felt to be unreliable, was interned in the Isle of Man, whence he later transferred to Stafford Gaol and Dartmoor. The Germans were led to suppose that MUTT was able to join the army and could therefore only transmit at intervals; JEFF, owing to his peculiar qualifications, was supposed to have obtained a position as interpreter at interrogations of refugees from Norway. He fell into trouble and was supposed to have been handed over to the Norwegian military authorities and sent in the autumn to Iceland. Relations with the Germans remained reasonably good until October, when wireless communication ceased for more than a month, probably because the Germans had lost confidence in their agents; but at the end of November the sabotage at Wealdstone restored the Germans' confidence, and MUTT was able to continue his transmissions and appeared to stand well with his masters.

CARELESS was a Polish airman who was shot down by the Germans in 1939, subsequently lived in France, found his way to Spain, and there got into touch with the Germans. His case was complicated by the fact that he was denounced by three Polish companions after his voyage to this country in July 1941, but he succeeded in establishing himself and communicated with the Germans by secret writing. CARELESS was considered to be difficult and temperamental; but he promised well as a double agent. His questionnaire was concerned mainly with the supply of aeroplanes to England from the United States, including the methods and routes by which they were brought here. He was also asked for general information about the R.A.F. in Britain, and in November he received a letter urging him to get into an armament factory and obtain production figures and so forth there. His traffic, however, was particularly concerned with A.A. defences, since he was notionally placed by us in the balloon barrage. He had considerable success in building up the A.A. defences in general and the balloon barrage in particular, and was thus able to instil into the Germans a wholesome fear of the strength of our passive defences.

FATHER, who arrived in England in June of 1941, was a distinguished Belgian pilot, who got into touch with the Germans in Belgium with the hope that he would be able to escape from the country by subterfuge. It was first proposed that he should go on behalf of the Germans to the United States; but he failed to obtain a visa and eventually travelled from Portugal to this country. His primary task was to work his way into the R.A.F., steal a plane, and fly it back to Occupied France. When it was intended that he should go to America, he was given times and frequencies suitable for communication from there, and he was told that he would have no difficulty in securing a transmitter himself in America. He also had secret ink for writing letters. In this country, as he could not develop secret writing, he wrote to the Germans and said that he would listen at the times and on the frequencies given him for America, but in fact these would have been unsuitable for transmissions to this country. The Germans therefore had no effective means of communication with him; but they solved this problem by communicating with DRAGON-FLY, who was instructed to communicate with FATHER. This was done by telephone, and in spite of the difficulties which arose owing to the fact that neither could well understand the other's language, DRAGONFLY succeeded in conveying to FATHER a new set of frequencies and times of transmission so that he could receive direct wireless messages from the Germans. His replies were sent by secret writing, though he was instructed in case of urgency to send replies through DRAGONFLY.

The case presented points of very great interest. In the first place, the method of communication (incoming messages by wireless and outgoing by secret writing) was extremely secure. Secondly, FATHER, as a highly skilful pilot, was in a position to discuss and report on technical developments in aircraft. His knowledge and skill, though they made him valuable, caused extreme difficulty to the approving authorities, who were naturally anxious lest he should give away too much. As he was keenly anxious to pursue his career as a pilot, it was also necessary to post him very carefully, since no one could be sure at the outset that he would not in fact go bad on us and even perhaps steal his aeroplane and return to France. In fact he was entirely loyal, but this fact could not be established beyond qusetion at the time, and he was therefore a cause of great anxiety. It was also impossible to allow him to send over any obvious misinformation, since his wife and children were in German hands and were being paid by them.

In the lower ranks SCRUFFY, a Belgian seaman, who arrived in September with a good quality secret ink and a cover address in Lisbon, was placed notionally in a coasting vessel in British waters and impersonated by a nominee of ours. His traffic was run in an obviously bogus fashion in order, as we hoped, to convince the Germans that we ran a double cross very badly. In this way we hoped to cover up some of the other agents. Unfortunately the Germans seemed unable to realise that SCRUFFY was obviously controlled and the case had therefore to be dropped.

SWEET WILLIAM, a British subject employed at the Spanish embassy, had the job of preparing summaries of the news for transmission to Spain. He was recruited by the colourful Spanish adventurer Alcazar, and was used by us to send espionage reports through the Spanish diplomatic bag. THE SNARK, a Yugoslav domestic servant, arrived in July after an unsuccessful attempt to return to Yugoslavia. Her training and capabilities confined her to the reporting of the prices of foodstuffs and similar information. Curiously, the ink which she was given was of high grade. BASKET, an Irishman, was landed near Dublin by parachute, also in July. He had two radio sets, over £400, and a good secret ink, and was highly qualified to act as a double agent, for he travelled to North Ireland and surrendered himself to the authorities there. Unfortunately his primary mission was to transmit weather reports from Sligo, and this, for obvious reasons, could not be permitted. He was therefore abandoned as a wireless agent, though attempts were made to run him as a letter-writing agent only.

Many other newcomers were tried and found wanting, but it would be fair to say that by the end of 1941 the team of double agents was strong and well balanced and that new recruits had more than compensated for the losses among the older members.

8: DEVELOPMENTS IN 1942

The early part of 1942 was to some extent a period of frustration. Those who knew most about the working of double agents felt most strongly that the weapon in our hands was not being sufficiently used. If reference is made once more to the objects of the double-cross system on page 58, it can readily be understood that the counterespionage objects had been to a large extent achieved but that very little had been done, compared to what seemed possible, on the side of intelligence and deception. We felt increasingly convinced that insufficient attention was paid to the intelligence information which could be deduced from questionnaires, and still more that inadequate use was made of the system to pass over misinformation to the enemy and to practise deception upon him. Moreover, however efficiently M.I.5 and M.I.6 might control their agents, it was impossible for them to improve the work in these particular spheres of activity without more guidance from higher authority.

Efforts were made to secure directives from the service members of the Twenty Committee which would enable us to pursue a more aggressive policy. It was pointed out that, if indeed we controlled the German intelligence system in this country and were in almost daily communication by wireless with the Germans, it was inconceivable that we could not, if we used our imagination and ingenuity, affect German policy to our own advantage. A second criticism, made by the head of B.1.A, was that, as things had worked out, we were not really in touch with the proper higher authorities. In his view, if the system was to be actively used, we ought to have been attached to Operations rather than (or as well as) to Intelligence in order that we might effectively further operational plans by deceptive methods.

The attempt to secure better directives was not very successful. On the civil side, the policy of Home Defence Executive was necessarily defensive, and their directive therefore amounted to little more than an instruction to us to avoid giving accurate information about damage to industrial objectives whenever possible and to avoid pinpointing industrial objectives. Civilian morale was to be written up as far as possible, although in fact evidences of high morale would be the last things that a real spy would report. Though, therefore, H.D.E. was a firm supporter of the system and anxious to build up the agents for the future, it could help us very little at the beginning of 1942.

The War Office also wished morale, training, equipment, and so forth to be written up as far as possible and considered it the wrong moment to embark on more exciting plans. Home Forces pointed out clearly that it was useless to control the enemy's espionage system if the danegeld of good information was too high; that since operational plans were still fluid, it was difficult to use the agents adequately for misinformation; and that, in consequence, we ought to consider whether better results would not be achieved by abandoning the agents and giving the enemy the difficult or impossible task of building up a new system of agents altogether.

The R.A.F. had produced one clear and workable directive in November of 1941, to which allusion has already been made in the preceding chapter. This directive instructed us to stress the great number of training crashes and the poor standard of training; to attempt to draw aerial attack away from towns and onto aerodromes; to give no information on aerodromes under construction; and to belittle the performance of new types of aircraft and engines. An additional directive instructed us to remark on the increasing tendency to mix types of aircraft; to spread the area used by our bomber forces; to remark on the mining of aerodromes; and to state that the satellites were receiving heavy ground defences; to state that ground defences on aerodromes and satellites were being improved and that the aircraft were being dispersed wherever possible away from perimeters. This was all to give the impression that there was a very large number of aircraft but that they were highly vulnerable when on the perimeters. These directives were extremely useful, but unfortunately they were not followed up by other and similar instructions.

The Admiralty policy was clearly stated. We were required to pass as much accurate information as possible for as many agents as possible, with a view to building them up for later deception or cover. In the meantime we were to put over *ad hoc* deceptions* and to give the enemy advance information of defensive measures which we were adopting before such measures were actually put into practice, in order to deter the enemy from attacks. In addition we were to magnify the strength of escorts, the armaments of our ships, and the effectiveness of our weapons.

None of these policy statements were in themselves sufficient to remove the strong impression that we had prepared a weapon of war and that it was not being fully used. It was felt that the approving authorities on the Twenty Committee were deteriorating into a body of censors whose chief function seemed to be to cut out or veto a large part of the information which we prepared for the agents. Naturally we were prepared to see much cut out, but it did not appear that sufficient advantage was being reaped from the work that was being put in. Stated otherwise, it seemed that we were sinking into a condition of playing for safety and building up an organisation which, so far as we could see, might never be used. How was it possible to transmit effective misinformation when we did not know what had to be concealed and when there was not even a consistent deception plan which we could support?

---

*In the event the Admiralty used double agents for a number of "*ad hoc* deceptions." Some of them are mentioned in chapter 12.

Nevertheless, on a long view, the cautious policy of the approving authorities on the Twenty Committee was clearly correct. A vivid and correct imagination, though it sees clearly the course of future events, almost invariably antedates results. Premature activity might well have wrecked our undertakings. The War Office and the Home Forces representatives pointed out that we were still on the defensive and that the great gains of deception could only be garnered when we passed to the offensive. In a defensive phase the chief merit was concealment, in an offensive phase the misinformation which we could pass to the enemy— but for this it was highly necessary to build up the agents so that the enemy had complete confidence in them. They would then be really valuable when the time for deception came. In other words we must keep our eye firmly fixed on time in the future when we should be able to put over large schemes of strategic deception, and we must remember that the gains from smaller pieces of tactical deception or from minor pieces of misinformation passed to the enemy were of small account when compared with the much more important though still distant objects.

Everything, therefore, pointed to one conclusion. There must be a powerful centralised control of strategic deception with a carefully planned policy, and the Controlling Officer of Deception must be someone fully apprised of all operational plans and fully informed also of all the weapons at his command for passing over his cover plan or deception. Our discontents, which were natural and probably inevitable, could be dissolved if deception were controlled and practised in the manner suggested above. Without such control of deception our efforts must be spasmodic and ineffective; but with a highly placed officer at the head of deception our organisation might become of the highest importance and the greatest value. Such a solution was, both in theory and in practice, far better than the proposal that we should be transferred bodily to Operations. The counterespionage and intelligence side of our work had to continue, and it would have been a complicated and difficult task to indoctrinate Operations with the whole history and theory of double agents, and in particular to convince them of the long build-up which was necessary. Operations would probably tend to sacrifice agents for short-term objectives, whereas the major value of the double agent system is the long-term use of the well-established agent.*

Meantime certain minor improvements were made in our system. We discovered that, though the volume of such questions was not large, there were a certain number of political questions with which none of our approving authorities were in fact competent to deal. In our efforts to expand the usefulness of the organisation we suggested that we could be of great service to P.W.E. For example, if messages were sent over containing reports from Italian prisoners, dissension might be sown between Italy and Germany. There was no theoretical reason why the double agent weapon should not be as effective in political as in military warfare. This proposal did not work out in the manner which we had hoped, but we did secure that Mr. Cavendish-Bentinck at the Foreign Office (who was also chairman of the Joint Intelligence Committee) should be empowered to approve political traffic for us, and this proposal was approved by the W. Board. Political traffic in fact never played a large part in our activities; but it was useful when padding was needed and when the status of certain agents had to be raised. Mr. Cavendish-Bentinck continued to assist us in this manner until the conclusion of the war.

Attempts to develop technical and scientific deception, which we made on several occasions, usually broke down owing to the difficulties inherent in this particular subject. A much more important point was that the Committee was put by the action of the Chief of the Secret Service (C.S.S.) in a position to act more effectively. Up to June of 1942

---

*An examination of the problem revealed a number of overwhelming objections to the suggestion that a double agent system should be run by Operations rather than by Intelligence. The argument is too long to be developed here.

only service members of the Committee, and of course the representatives of M.I.5 and M.I.6, were allowed to have official cognisance of certain secret sources. H.D.E. and Home Forces were kept in official ignorance of them, and this made some of the discussions unreal, since it was impossible to discuss the reliability and use of agents when some of those participating in the discussion were not in possession of the most relevant evidence. Consequently a letter was written on behalf of the Committee to C.S.S., who replied giving his approval to the proposal that all members of the Committee should have these secret sources (in so far as they concerned double agents or their work) made available to them.

Further improvements were made in July. With a view to increasing the efficiency of the work on another side, the W. Board arranged that each of the services should free an officer for full-time or almost full-time double-cross activities, and that General Eisenhower and Admiral Stark respectively should be approached in order that an individual American officer in the army and the navy should be appointed by them for approving information connected with the American forces. Earlier in the year a proposal from M.I.6 that "blown" sets of their agents should be handed over to the Twenty Committee had opened up a new field of work. On the whole, though much time was devoted to these cases, little advantage was obtained from them, perhaps because we failed to use them imaginatively enough to obtain German intelligence information from them.

Let us return to the main argument. The double agent system had been built up and was in full running order. It had achieved some successes, particularly on the side of security and counterespionage. It was being wasted, as we thought, on the side of deception. This could only be corrected by the establishment of a proper deception control and by convincing the chiefs of Deception of the value of our organisation. Fortunately the possibilities of organising deception were clear to more important persons also.

The real home of successful deception was the Middle

East. There it really developed early in 1942, and, more fortunately still, double agents were used to assist it. CHEESE, a famous double agent of the Middle East, had been apparently blown in 1941, but was built up again and became once more effective in the summer of 1942. In this country Colonel Stanley had been appointed Controlling Officer of Deception by the Chiefs of Staff with a view to coordinating all strategic deception under them in October of 1941. It was, however, decided by the W. Board that he should not be informed of the double agents, but that he should only be told that we had certain opportunities of passing information to the Germans. One of his hands, therefore, was tied behind his back from the start. From the Middle East in 1942 Lord Wavell pressed for an energetic use of long-distance deception and for the active use of deception plans. This pressure from such a quarter was probably the real turning point.

In May of 1942 Colonel Bevan succeeded Colonel Lumley as staff officer to the Controlling Officer of Deception, and in June he became himself Controlling Officer. It is fair, therefore, to say that by the early summer of 1942 strategic deception was fairly launched in this country as well as in the Middle East. Our position was that we had ready an instrument which had been tried and tested and which we could offer to the Controlling Officer for use in his deception plans. It became our business not, as it had been in the past, to promote and press through small plans of our own, but to provide channels for deception according to the plans of the Controlling Officer. In addition, of course, it was necessary for us to arrange the lives of our agents in such a way that they would be most useful for deception and to give a clear judgment in every case as to whether any individual agent could or could not carry out the particular task which the Controlling Officer wished to see done.

Like almost every other wartime institution, the control of deception grew up gradually in accordance with the needs. Theoretically some such organisation could have

been created, if sufficient prior thought had been given to
the matter, at the beginning of the war; but it must be
doubtful if the event in that case would have been as successful as it was. A great deal of experience had been gained
by our own small efforts and plans, and we had a tolerably
exact knowledge of what a double agent could or could not
do in such matters. As things were, the double agent system
played probably a greater part than it would have done if a
cut-and-dried deception plan and deception staff had existed
from the beginning of the war. An incident in the spring
had brought out very clearly the difficulties of the situation
prior to Colonel Bevan's appointment.

In May Lord Swinton had proposed that there should be
discussions with Lord Louis Mountbatten about the possibility of using our agents in connection with the Isle of
Wight. It was suggested that DRAGONFLY, if moved down
to the neighbourhood, could give the Germans sufficient
information to prevent them from creating new sources of
information there, and that the operations of C.C.O. from
the island could thus be effectively covered. This plan did
not mature, for the reasons with which we were by then
only too familiar; but it is certain that had deception been
developed and organised by then, a cover plan for operations in the south could have been worked out and passed
to the Germans. It is sad, but interesting, to speculate
whether the Dieppe raid might not have been more successful, or at least less costly, if it had been effectively covered.

When finally the control of deception was firmly established and our main handicap thus removed, we were in
some danger of rushing to the opposite extreme and sacri-
ficing everything to deception. In August 1942, D.N.I. cir-
cularised the members of the W. Board, suggesting that the
activities of the Twenty Committee would be more profitable if the Committee were placed directly under the Controlling Officer of Deception, who would be in touch with
the requirements of the Chiefs of Staff and the Joint Planners. He suggested that Colonel Bevan should be appointed
chairman of the Committee, and in fact that the whole double
agent system should be run as an offshoot of deception.

Colonel Bevan himself had no wish for this change. He very reasonably regarded double agents as a channel through which his deception could be passed, and he did not desire to control agents himself or to busy himself with the details of the agents' lives. The W. Board also kept its head and reaffirmed its belief that the double-cross system was useful for counterespionage and intelligence as well as for deception. It also agreed that the Security Service and M.I.6 were normally the best judges as to how the machine under their control could be put into motion to the best advantage. Consequently, and happily, the organisation remained unchanged: but the Twenty Committee was fortified by the addition of Colonel Bevan and of a representative from C.C.O.

The benefits accruing to the general interest were not slow in coming, for already by November 1942 the first organised piece of strategic deception from this country had been carried out. The deception referred to was the cover plan for the landings in North Africa—in other words, the plan to cover Operation TORCH. It is not our business here or elsewhere in this narrative to write the history of deception; but it is necessary to allude briefly to the objects of some of the deception plans in order to explain how and why double agents were used.

To cover TORCH there were two main plans, SOLO 1 and OVERTHROW, which were initiated at the end of July and the objects of which were to threaten landings in Norway and on the north coast of France respectively. At the end of August, when the plans had been agreed and passed, it was settled that FATHER, MUTT and JEFF, TATE, GARBO, DRAGONFLY, CARELESS, BALLOON, and GELATINE should be the agents used, and a variety of items of information were allotted to them from which the Germans might deduce the time and place of our attacks.* TORCH was a highly successful operation, and, judging solely by results, the fullest credit must be given to strategic deception for

---

*There was also a plan, or series of plans, to cover the build-up at Gibraltar by implying that this was for the reinforcement of Malta, which was pictured as being in desperate straits.

this success, for the landings on 8 November were an entire
surprise to the Germans. Nevertheless it must be admitted
that the success was not primarily a triumph for deception,
and still less for the double agent system.

The threatened attacks on Norway and the north of
France, though they may have had some effect, were not
the chief factors in deceiving the Germans. It seems rather
to be true that the Germans deceived themselves. Their
basic error was the belief that we had not the shipping
available for an operation of the magnitude of that undertaken. As the situation developed, they expected an attack
somewhere, but not on the scale of the actual operation;
and on the whole they expected this attack to take place at
Dakar. On 16 November the Turkish ambassador in Rome
said that the Germans there had been definitely of the
opinion that the concentration of forces in Gibraltar immediately prior to the recent attack had been intended for
an attack on Dakar, and that they never thought that the
blow would fall inside the Mediterranean. The suggestion
of Dakar seems to have come from German inspired sources
and not from England. The real triumph of TORCH from our
angle was *not* that the cover plans were successfully planted
on the Germans but what the real plan was not disclosed
or guessed. In other words, it was a triumph of security.

From the point of view of the double agent system there
was, however, both much to be learnt from this operation
and considerable cause of satisfaction. We learned that in
many cases we should assist deception most by securing
that dangerous information did *not* pass to the enemy, rather
than by passing misinformation. With regard to the misinformation, the fact that the Gibraltar stories went well and
the Norwegian and French stories less well underlined the
obvious fact that cover schemes ought to be as near the
"real thing" as was safely possible.

Fortunately, and certainly, the position of the agents
themselves was not jeopardised. The first reaction on the
German side may have been that they had been badly informed; but on second thoughts they must have come to

the conclusion that the agents had not really done badly. If cover plans (and the Germans must have been beginning to guess that cover plans were used by us) such as attacks on Norway and on northern France were mounted in this country, the agents from their observations would be deceived as much as everybody else. The troops participating did not themselves know the scene of the actual operation, and it was therefore entirely natural and right that the agents also should be deceived about the actual objectives. Except when certain specific questions were asked, the agents had confined themselves to facts, and when they had stated opinions they had not really let themselves down. Thus DRAGONFLY, who was asked on 18 October: "Have you the impression that new operation is being prepared? Atlantic or Africa?" had replied: "Several soldiers believe soon attack like Dieppe, but bigger, against north coast France. On south coast no signs of operation in Atlantic or against Africa, but a lot of newspaper talk and rumours about Dakar." It would have been unreasonable if a man in his position had not been deceived by the cover plan on the south coast, and the Germans could hardly give him a bad mark for that.

Certainly the Germans must have realised after TORCH that extensive cover plans were used, and consequently they might be expected to require more detailed and more factual information in the future, so that they could judge for themselves whether troop movements and the like were concerned with cover or real operations.

Once more one part of this narrative has run ahead of the rest; the development of strategic deception has been carried down to the autumn of 1942, the history of the agents and their work must now be brought from the end of 1941, which it had reached in chapter 7, up to the end of 1942. Nor must one warning be forgotten. As strategic deception increased in importance the other parts of our work did not diminish but increased proportionately.

If it is accepted that the most important task of the agents was to pass over (or, to use the horrid language of officialdom, "implement") the plans of deception, it must also be admitted that this was best done against the background of a general reporting agency. You cannot baldly *announce* to the enemy that such and such an operation is in preparation or that such and such a division is being trained to invade North Africa or Norway. What you have to do— granted that you control the major part of the German intelligence service—is to send over a great deal of factual information, introducing into it those facts from which the German intelligence staff will deduce your (deception) intentions. Moreover, you cannot just volunteer information. The agent's first duty is to answer questions passed by the Germans, and therefore you must by your answers guide subsequent questions in the direction you desire. Consequently the main tasks before us were (1) to maintain an efficient though changing team of agents, which constituted the German intelligence service here; (2) to keep up a steady stream of information, mainly true, which would satisfy the Germans; (3) so to manœuvre our agents that

they should be both rightly placed geographically and concerned with matters which could be turned to account in
order that we should be able (4) to introduce the deception
information plausibly when deception required us to do so.

First, then, the position of the team in 1942. The year
began with a major disaster, for G.W. was lost in February.
The reasons for his demise were neither our fault nor of our
seeking. He had succeeded in "implementing" his own
second resurrection in June 1941, when he had got into
touch with Calvo at the Spanish embassy, and through him
had passed a number of documents of high importance.
Unfortunately the Spaniards were working a considerable
espionage organisation in this country; in this Calvo was
involved, and it was decided to arrest him as part of a plan
to clear up this espionage ring. We dissented, of course,
from the proposed action, but our protests did not prevail.
Calvo was arrested and G.W.'s career as a double agent
was ended. The loss to us was great, for he was by far the
best channel we ever had for the transmission of documents,
and his value in this respect might have been a growing
asset. Moreover, his "elimination" placed others of our
agents in danger and imposed a policy of extreme caution
upon us. It is permissible to suggest that at a later stage,
when the reputation of the double agent system was more
firmly established and its uses better understood, our view
would have prevailed. As things were we were compelled
to make the best of a bad job and continue with a depleted
team.

Fortunately there were a number of new cases which
more than filled the gaps in the team. Some of them were
only of passing interest, whilst others presented new and
interesting features. PEPPERMINT, a Catalan, who was employed at the Spanish embassy for press purposes and as
a courier, had fallen under the influence of Alcazar, and
was instructed by him to send reports in secret ink from this
country through the Spanish diplomatic bag. These reports,
which were partially controlled, were used both for the
Germans and for the Japanese in the Peninsula.

In April a new development occurred in Iceland. The capture of an Icelandic steamer sending reports by wireless to the Germans and the landing of COBWEB from a submarine enabled us to create an effective channel to the Germans from that island. COBWEB's set was operated from the Admiral's house, and two somewhat elaborate plans were attempted under Admiralty control; the first, to bring out the German fleet at a time when it could be dealt with adequately by our Home Fleet, and the second, to divert the enemy from the Russian convoys. The deception side of the second plan was tolerably successful, and M.I.6 continued to operate COBWEB until the end of the war. He was joined in September 1943 by BEETLE, who was also landed from a U-boat. Both were useful in a number of ways, e.g., as good security and counterespionage checks, and for sending out a number of messages about naval movements which it was desired to pass to the Germans. They also had their share in later strategic deception plans. Distance from headquarters and complications with the Americans, who of course at a later stage had to be put into the picture, together with difficulties over weather reports (on which the Germans were insistent), made it difficult to extract the full value from these Icelandic agents; nevertheless they played their part in the general scheme.

In April also GARBO was brought to this country. He had already been working for some nine months as a kind of free-lance double agent in Lisbon, but he was now smuggled to England and started his activities here under our control. Connoisseurs of double cross have always regarded the GARBO case as the most highly developed example of their art, interesting alike for the illustrations which it gives of all the many sides of the work, for the skill and ingenuity with which it was controlled by its case officer, and for the efficiency with which all possible advantages were squeezed from it. GARBO, therefore, plays a leading part in all the later part of this narrative. If in the double-cross world SNOW was the W.G. Grace of the early period, then GARBO was certainly the Bradman of the later years.

The case was unique in that GARBO himself, rejected by our officials abroad and playing a lone hand, imposed himself upon the Germans and himself performed the difficult operation of creating and establishing his own trusty and trusted espionage agency. He came to us therefore a fully fledged double agent with all his growing pains over—we had only to operate and develop the system which he had already built up.

GARBO was a Spaniard, equally hostile to communism and fascism. During the civil war he was compelled to hide, remaining immured in one house for a period of two years. When the world war started it occurred to his inventive mind that he might obtain employment as a British agent in either Germany or Italy. His offer was rejected in January 1941, and he therefore conceived the bolder project of offering himself to the Germans with a view to double-crossing them. Once recruited by them his value to the British, so he argued, would be sensibly increased. The event was ultimately to justify his expectations. He was well received by the Germans in the embassy in Madrid and, after characteristically lengthy and involved negotiations, he persuaded them that he could contrive to be sent by the Spaniards on a mission to England. To this end he forged a Spanish diplomatic document and departed from Madrid in July 1941 with a questionnaire, secret ink, money, cover addresses, and the German blessing, notionally *en route* for England.

But for nine months he did not go to England at all. Instead he remained in Lisbon, whence he indited long and colourful letters to his German friends, supposedly written in England and conveyed by courier to Portugal for posting. These contained his espionage reports on the British Isles. He worked with indifferent tools: a Blue Guide, a map of England, an out-of-date railway timetable formed his stock in trade, supplemented by meagre gleanings from Portuguese bookstalls. But fiction suitably presented is often more easily credible than truth, and it was not long before the Germans came to trust his reports and to appreciate them highly. Moreover, GARBO played his game with masterly skill. When his railway timetable told him that some line was important owing to the amount of traffic passing along it, he defended that line with newly erected wire and pillboxes cunningly camouflaged. When the Germans asked him to find out if armoured units had been observed moving south in Hertfordshire and Bedfordshire, he did not forget a little later to report just such units passing southward through Guildford. To assist him he created three subagents, who reported to him from the west country, from Glasgow, and from Liverpool.

Since he always reported what the Germans expected to hear, and since many of his guesses were startlingly near to the truth, he was more and more readily believed. None the less GARBO's existence was precarious in the extreme. He had so little knowledge of English ways and English habits that he remained permanently poised on the edge of a precipice over which some blunder or other must, as it seemed, soon impel him. He could, for example, not convert pence into shillings or shillings into pounds, and so the early expense accounts of his subagents present a problem to students of the curious; again, he knew almost no English names, and so his postbox in Lisbon carried the all-British legend "Mr. Smith-Jones."

But such trifling difficulties as these did not unduly alarm him. Once his correspondence was in full swing he made further attempts to offer his services to the British authorities, only to experience again the cold rebuffs of officialdom. But he succeeded in December 1941 in getting into touch with a neutral diplomat, and in February 1942 some account of GARBO's activities percolated to this country. At about the same time secret sources revealed that the Germans were making elaborate preparations to intercept a large convoy which was supposed to have left Liverpool for Malta. Only later did we establish the fact that GARBO was the sole inventor and begetter of this convoy, and thus responsible for a great expenditure of useless labour on the part of the enemy. It became clear to us at this stage that

GARBO was more fitted to be a worthy collaborator than an unconscious competitor. In April 1942, therefore, he was smuggled across to England, and continued from this country the work which he had notionally already performed from here since July of the preceding year.

The case developed enormously in this country, and GARBO soon controlled an active and well-distributed team of imaginary assistants, some of whom wrote directly to the Germans, though all received their answers, orders, and questionnaires through the head of the organisation. Among the original subagents there was one early casualty. When Operation TORCH was pending it seemed that agent No. 2, who lived in Liverpool and from whom GARBO had received notice of his Malta convoy, was in a position to see more than was desirable. Accordingly he became afflicted with a lingering malady and ceased to send in his reports. Much perturbed, GARBO hurried north and from there informed the Germans that the poor man had died. An obituary notice inserted by us in the *Liverpool Daily Post* was duly conveyed to the Germans, who expressed their profound sympathy with the widow. The other two subagents of the original creation remained, and to these four more were added—a Gibraltarian waiter; a brother of agent No. 3 who was eventually to go to Canada; a F.S.P. who was sent to North Africa; and a seaman whose main use was to arrange notionally for such documents and espionage material to be conveyed to Lisbon as in fact travelled in the M.I.6 bag.

In May the WEASEL, a Belgian doctor, fell into our hands, and it appeared likely that he would be a valuable addition, for he had been trained in secret writing and w/t and was a man of experience and intelligence. Unfortunately his secret letters received no reply, and it was thought likely that the WEASEL contrived to insert some secret warning to the Germans that he was under control. In June another promising case, that of CARROT, a Luxembourger, also failed to develop, owing partly to complications over his dealings with the Deuxième Bureau, and WASHOUT, son

of a night watchman in the British embassy at Lisbon, who
was also sent here, turned out to be by temperament and
ability unsuited to play any satisfactory part.

Much more interesting and important was the case of
HAMLET and the other agents connected with him. Our
connection with HAMLET was made through MULLET, a
British subject born in Belgium of a British father and a
Belgian mother, who had lived for most of his life in
Belgium. MULLET spent two months in Lisbon at the end
of 1941 on his way back to this country and was introduced
there to HAMLET, an Austrian ex-cavalry officer, a Jew, a
businessman, and an exploiter of various commercial
patents.

As HAMLET entertained MULLET, who was a new acquaintance of his, some twenty or twenty-five times to
dinner, it was a fair assumption that he was anxious to
make use of him in some way or other. In fact, HAMLET
wished MULLET to do three things: to take jewelery over
to his two children, whom he had sent to England before
the war; to act as HAMLET's business representative in this
country; and, most important of all, to discover what opportunities there were for transmitting peace feelers to
England and for assisting those persons in Germany who
were anxious to break away from Nazi domination and to
secure a peace. HAMLET, in fact, declared as early as 1941
that there was strong military opposition to Hitler, and that
he himself believed that this opposition could be assisted
and made effective for the benefit of the Allies as well as of
Germany. At a later stage it became evident that HAMLET
was actually himself employed by the Abwehr, though his
position with it did not become at all important until later.
He became the centre of the so-called Kolberg Organisation,
an enterprise controlled by Ast Brussels, which operated
in Lisbon under commercial cover and which was a source
of great jealousy to K.O. Lisbon.

MULLET reported all HAMLET's ideas and proposals to
us, and in August 1942 he was sent out to Lisbon again
for further conversations with HAMLET. The latter asked

that we should supply him with information for his work, but made the rather startling suggestion that all the information which we should give him should be information which would indicate the strength of Great Britain, particularly with regard to the bombing of Germany, in order that the hands of those opposing Hitler should be strengthened. Clearly the case offered great opportunity for political warfare, for it provided a channel whereby we could be reasonably sure that information about our power and resources would reach the right quarters in Germany. It was not, however, considered wise at that time to use this particular opportunity with energy; on the other hand, it was decided to maintain the case for future use. At a later date PUPPET, an associate of HAMLET's and a friend of Von Falkenhausen's, the then governor of Occupied Belgium, was sent over to represent HAMLET's commercial interests in this country.

As a double-cross case HAMLET, MULLET, and PUPPET represented a highly attractive proposition and in some ways a unique opportunity. For purposes of information MULLET and PUPPET could be supplied by us and could pass their information to HAMLET under an elaborate business cover. This business cover was the branch of HAMLET's Portuguese company which was established in this country (and which compelled B.1.A to embark on considerable business activities connected with soaps, impregnated paper, and degreasing patents, as well as lemonade powder). The unique opportunity was that HAMLET, who was really himself a double-cross agent, was actually a member of the Abwehr, and we could therefore be sure that our information reached its goal and that it would in all probability be believed.

There were, however, certain drawbacks, which prevented us from drawing a proper dividend from the case. In the first place, the opportunities which it offered to other departments made us chary of using the case fully for our own ends; secondly, HAMLET's own motives were for a long time suspect, and he was not built up as he should have been by an adequate supply of information in the early days; and thirdly, we were unable to get as much information about him from other sources as we did in the case of other agents. As a result, full advantage was not taken of the opportunities presented, though some advantage was reaped from it at a later stage.

In the autumn more recruits were added. JOSEF, a Russian, who had been detained for some time at the Oratory Schools, had become friendly with Matsumoto, formerly honorary press attaché to the Japanese embassy. JOSEF, as a seaman, visited Lisbon and made his way to the Japanese legation there. He thus made a link with the Japanese. He and other seamen agents of the same kind were never an entirely satisfactory part of the double-cross system. It is true that they established a useful link by personal contact with the Germans and Japanese at Lisbon, but in the nature of things they could not be properly controlled. However reliable we might consider such an agent, and however carefully he might be coached, it still remained true that a seafaring man might well, when questioned, give away a great deal, particularly about convoys, which we desired to suppress. Nor, again, could we be at all certain that he would accurately convey to the enemy the misinformation which we had given him. In fact, as much harm as good might well be done by a seaman agent of this kind.

In October BRONX, the daughter of a South American diplomat, established herself with us as a very competent letter-writing agent. She had accomplished a mission to France for the British in July to October 1942, and on her return reported that she had been in touch with enemy intelligence service, who had recruited her to report on industrial affairs. She was promised a salary of £100 a month, which was afterwards paid with satisfactory regularity, though for a time it appeared that the Germans had no great interest in her. In the same month TRICYCLE returned to this country from America and started a new phase in his activities, and BRUTUS, a Polish agent who turned out to be extremely important, also reached England. His case will be explained in the next chapter.

Another valuable addition was LIPSTICK, a Catalan much concerned with the Catalan Separatist movement. He discussed with Cornudella, the leader in Barcelona of the Catalan movement, the possibility of travelling to England in order to get in touch with the Catalan movement here, and with this object he approached some German friends who might, he thought, assist him to obtain the necessary papers. The Germans, who were deceived about LIPSTICK's history and views, agreed to assist him on condition that he should act as a German agent in England. He reported to the British embassy in Madrid what had happened, and it was agreed to facilitate his journey here. He had lessons in secret writing from the Germans, and received from them materials for writing, a microscope and developer for secret writing, and six cover addresses to which he could write. LIPSTICK was therefore a singularly well-equipped letter-writing agent, and his training and experience made him fully competent to report on matters connected with production, industry, and science. The weak point in the case was that his own first interest was to further the Catalan movement rather than to assist us.

In November WATCHDOG was landed from a U-boat in Canada together with a wireless set and an extensive questionnaire. This move on the part of the Germans threatened an extension of our activities to other parts of the world, but in fact the case did not develop very satisfactorily. A little later in December a South African scientist who had been suborned by the Germans in a concentration camp in France reached this country and was arrested. He confessed, and it was arranged that he should return to South Africa, and act as a double agent operating a wireless set from there—a task for which his scientific knowledge and his desire to rehabilitate himself made him peculiarly well-fitted. In this case, however, the South African government for security reasons finally refused to allow the experiment to be made in South Africa.

Finally, in December ZIGZAG landed in this country. He was a criminal who had been imprisoned in Jersey for safe-blowing and similar activities, had been taken over by the Germans when they occupied the island, had offered his services to them in order, as he alleged, to escape to this country, and who had been carefully trained by the Germans in sabotage and in radio transmission at Nantes. He was dropped by parachute near Ely, bringing with him an intelligence questionnaire and a wireless set. He immediately handed himself over and told his story with apparent candour and completeness.

In fact we knew a great deal about ZIGZAG before his arrival, and elaborate preparations had been made with regional and police authorities to secure him quickly and without advertisement as soon as he arrived. Details of his training had been discovered from secret sources. We even knew that he could be identified by certain false teeth, because his departure from France had been postponed as the result of an accident during his parachute training, and the dental repairs had found their place in secret sources. We knew indeed a great deal about him; we knew that he would be in possession of two identity cards; we knew the details of his equipment, and we knew that an act of sabotage would be his primary assignment. What we did not know was whether he was really on our side or on that of the Germans. His behaviour and demeanour on arrival convinced us that he was on ours.

ZIGZAG's case was of absorbing interest for a variety of reasons. He had been most carefully trained even to the extent of having practice in being dropped by parachute. He had worked for a long period in the Nantes Stelle and had, therefore, a fund of information about enemy radio transmissions. The tasks set him were first and foremost to sabotage the de Havilland works at Hatfield where Mosquito light bombers were made. On this the Germans placed the greatest importance. In addition he was to send daily weather reports, particulars of the movement of American troops, and information about American divisional signs and shipbuilding. He was also to report on internal transport in this country. For all these purposes he had been supplied with £1,000 and explosive materials. What made his case particularly interesting was that his work was to be completed in a few weeks, and he was then to return either by shipping as a seaman to Portugal, or by way of Ireland, or by means of a submarine which was to be sent for him. He was promised £15,000 for the de Havilland sabotage, and was told if he brought it off and returned, the Germans would probably send him to control a special sabotage undertaking in the United States.

The case therefore presented new features and new problems. If full advantage was to be taken of it, ZIGZAG would have (apparently at least) to carry out his act of sabotage, and also return to the Germans. If he did this he might be able to communicate with us from Nantes, and we might also control and prevent extensive sabotage by German agents in America; but it was essential, if he were to return, that he should not know or guess at the knowledge which we had through secret sources. The possibility had at all times to be considered that he might, on return to enemy territory, be persuaded or forced to reveal his association with British intelligence. Speed was also a necessity. Dr. Graumann, who was ZIGZAG's spy-master, had shrewdly but perhaps unwisely told him that if he fell into British hands, and the British tried to use him, it would take a long time, for the Germans could rely on "red tape to stop the ball rolling." Consequently, a quick decision had to be made, and ZIGZAG was put on the air at once. His achievement and subsequent career belong to a later chapter.

By the end of 1942 therefore, in spite of some casualties, the team of agents was distinctly stronger in all departments than it had been a year previously. The work which they had done during the year requires a brief mention. The questions sent by the Germans had increased in volume, and had as before clearly reflected the German interests from month to month. Once again it is impossible to give a satisfactory summary of the questions or answers; it must suffice to indicate a few of the main interests. First and foremost the Germans had made any indications of British offensives the first claim on the agents. Quite obviously they had begun to think defensively, and they demanded not only general information about projected invasions, but also all sorts of details connected with concentrations and movement of troops, stoppage of leave, concentrations of small craft and equipment, and so forth, which might help them to prognosticate the time and place of any such invasion.

The next subject in order of importance, judged by German standards, was connected also with possible offensives. It was the subject of gliders, and airborne and parachute troops. Questions were asked about the details of the convoys and tactical use of an airborne division, details of transport gliders, their capacity, production figures, and so forth, and details also of new methods of landing and towing gliders. Our order of battle continued to be a matter of great interest. A captured German document, *Das Britische Kriegsheer*, dated April 1942, showed us up to a point what the Germans already knew, and their questions seemed to show that they were trying to fill up blanks and clear up dubious cases in this document. Consequently we knew where they could be deceived.

Other questions which had a high priority included the aircraft industry and new types of aircraft; and here again the questions indicated to us where the Germans' information was imperfect. Thus in July they asked questions about an underground aircraft factory said to be employing nearly eight thousand workers, but of which they did not know even the approximate location. Many technical aircraft details were also asked for. In August one agent was asked about aircraft guiding waves, Cockerel apparatus, the use of infrared equipment, and of radio location equipment called D.F.G.10. In the next month he was asked again for details of guiding waves, and for stations and squadron signs, Fleet Air Arm wireless equipment and frequencies, ASV., and the technical details of dive bombers such as automatic diving brakes and flattening-out control. In October the questions became more technical still.

Other questions which were obviously important included information about the American forces in the British Isles, the Canadian forces, and combined operations. In the last case the organisation, strength, and equipment of Commandos was asked for, and the location of Commandos Nos. 5, 6, 7, 11, and 12. With regard to tanks, they seemed to be more interested in production than in specifications, but an exception was the interest shown in the "crusher" tank. It was not known whence the Germans first heard of this tank, which in fact did not exist, but between March and July 1942 they made at least five attempts to obtain information about it.

Questions about other matters: production, food, convoys, gas, air raid damage, and so forth, continued as before, but there were remarkably few questions on naval matters. Probably, bearing in mind the clarity with which German interests and also German deficiencies in knowledge were exposed, we did not take the fullest advantage of our powers to deceive them. Nevertheless a useful stream of misinformation was passed to them together with true but innocuous information. With regard to production our policy of dispersal was well written up, and with regard to airborne troops our strength was carefully exaggerated. In October the Controlling Officer of Deception obtained from the Chiefs of Staff a directive according to which it was regarded as safe to exaggerate military strength by about 10 percent.

Various plans were put through as before, but their importance and interest was usually only ephemeral. The most ingenious of them, Plan PAPRIKA, designed to indicate a serious spirit of rebellion in the German Higher Command in the Low Countries, was never put into operation owing to doubts abouts its political wisdom. GARBO's finances were put in order by means of Plan DREAM, whereby certain Spanish fruit merchants paid money to us in England in return for pesetas paid by the Germans in Spain. Finally, MUTT and JEFF kept the home fires burning by means of an act of sabotage, Plan BROCK, in Hampshire. It had been arranged that some Nissen huts should be blown up with the connivance of Southern Command, for the same reasons which had previously induced us to undertake acts of sabotage. The usual difficulties occurred. The explosion was so effective that the tangible evidences of sabotage were destroyed, and the Norwegian compass which had been carefully left on the spot was stolen and disappeared. Some local sheep strayed too near the danger zone, and a soldier from a nearby camp was arrested and seemed unable to find any convincing story to exonerate himself. However, judicious planting of further clues and the intervention of a Special Branch officer sent by us brought local opinion round to the theory of sabotage, and appropriate accounts appeared in the local press.

10: ACTIVITIES IN 1943

It is difficult to recapture the changing thoughts, impressions, and moods of past years. Chiefly one remembers only that the road was long and that victory seemed to be always round the next corner. Certainly the great day when Western Europe would be invaded seemed throughout the middle years of the war much nearer than it was, and when the Germans' surrender at Stalingrad in January 1943 took place every optimist—and almost all were optimists, else how should we have worried through?—imagined that the stretch ahead would only be a short one.

Let us keep this in mind with reference to the double-cross system. If a fresh picture is permissible, we might think of a man who starts on a quarter-mile race; when he has run a couple of hundred yards those on the edge of the track shout to him that it is a half-mile race on which he has entered, and a little later it is borne in on him that the distance to be covered is a mile or perhaps three miles. Can he adapt himself, and will he last to the finish at all, let alone be in the lead when the last lap is run? So it was with the double-cross system.

It must be remembered that we had always looked forward to the day when we should take part in the great final deception which would pay ten times over for everything we had given out earlier. But no one can maintain a bluff indefinitely; sooner or later a blunder or sheer mischance will inevitably give it away. How should we feel if the whole of the double-cross system collapsed before it had been put to the test in a grand deception? The fear that this would happen was constantly in our mind, and was increased by the belief, which was probably at the worst only partially justified, that the collapse of one important case would destroy all the rest with it. If the Germans, so we thought, once gained full knowledge of our procedure in one important double-cross case, they would inevitably become suspicious of the rest, examine them in every detail, and end by guessing at the truth about them all. So our mood in 1943 was one of gnawing anxiety lest our opportunity should not come soon enough for us to use it. The double-cross runner might be lying exhausted at the side of the track and out of the race altogether when the bell actually rang for the last lap.

Fortunately, things turned out otherwise; the great day came; the grand deception succeeded; the double-cross agents played a not undistinguished part; but all that was in 1944 and not in 1943. Nor, though ultimate success excuses everything and banishes also doubts and hesitations to a decent oblivion, were our fears groundless. As will be shown in chapter 11, it was a near run thing. Probably, though this is surmise, our double-cross system only just lasted the course, and could hardly have done so had D Day been postponed, let us say, to the end of 1944. Luckily we can afford to forget how small the margin was.

Meantime we have to consider 1943, and this must be done shortly in order that the main course of the story may not be delayed or interrupted; but because it is treated shortly, it must not be thought that the period was uneventful or unimportant for us. On a sober appraisement it can well be argued that the most worthy though least showy achievement of B.1.A and the Twenty Committee was to keep the whole system running and functioning throughout the years 1942 and 1943, so that in fact it *was* still in place and ready to play its part in 1944.

The events of the year 1943 and the work done then may therefore be reduced to a brief summary under the headings of strategic deception, plans and minor pieces of tactical deception, and the affairs of the agents themselves. In deception we, as well as the Controlling Officer, encountered all the difficulties inherent in the task before us. A major operation has to be carefully planned and suffers as a rule many changes and amendments before it is finally passed by those in supreme authority—and this difficulty is enhanced when supreme authority is vested in an Allied rather than in a purely British command. Other difficulties occurred before the deception machine was running smoothly. Thus at one time the strength of British and American forces was being "written down" and at the same time "notional divisions" were being created, which had the effect of "writing up" our strength. The cover or deception plan cannot be devised until the real plan is communicated at least in outline to those in control of deception, and then in its turn the cover plan has to be accepted and approved. After that again the cover plan has constantly to be altered in detail to conform to the needs of the real plan, and sometimes it has to be scrapped altogether to meet the exigencies of a new situation. Consequently time was nearly always terribly short both for the Controlling Officer to work out and obtain approval for his plans, and for us on a lower level when we had to implement some of the details.

We suffered too in another way. Whereas in the early days we had lacked any detailed direction, we now often had too much. It was the business of double-cross agents to pass over facts and details to support their deception plans; these plans were worked out with the greatest care and elaboration, and all the moves were arranged in advance. Thus, for example, we would be told that on D minus 25 we should report that H.Q. of X Division had moved from the Eastern Counties to Scotland; or that on D minus 20 a convoy was to assemble at Liverpool. Our business was not to question the why or wherefor of such moves, but only to arrange that some agent or agents should be in a position to pass the report plausibly and convincingly, always remembering that the time for prior manœuvring of the agents was short and that the details of the plan might be switched round at a moment's notice.

In fact we succeeded in satisfying the demands of deception without "blowing" our agents, and without refusing any really urgent demand made on us. We always insisted that we could not implement anything which in our judgment would not be believed by the Germans, or would certainly "blow" the agent. This was a necessary precaution, for without it we might have been left without any agents when the time for invasion came.

The basic idea of the deception policy during 1943 up to the beginning of the winter was to "contain the maximum enemy forces in Western Europe and the Mediterranean area and thus discourage their transfer to the Russian front." For this purpose numerous threats of landings and invasions had to be made, and the double-cross agents assisted in all these matters. The most important of these was Operation STARKEY, the original object of which was "to mount a major amphibious feint against the Pas de Calais area in such a manner as to convince the enemy that a large-scale landing is imminent and so designed, without actually committing our land forces to an assault, as to compel the German fighter force to engage in air battles of attrition at times and places most advantageous to us." At a later stage the real part of the operation was abandoned, but the preparations were continued in the form of an exercise. Norway, too, was a favourite playground for deception, and even the most retentive memory would have difficulty in recalling just when and how often our agents helped to put into effect a threat against that country. The bulk of this work fell on MUTT and JEFF, who originated a threat in April, in August, and again in October of 1943. The details of these matters belong to the history of deception and cannot be recounted here.

Broadly speaking, deception was successful during the year, at least in its main objective of causing the Germans anxiety and doubt about the next blow. From our point of view the chief cause of satisfaction was that the agents survived with undiminshed prestige ready for the more important operations of the future. The organisation of deception underwent some change during the period, and these changes had repercussions on the double-cross system. In

June COSSAC was formed by General Morgan, and in the autumn General Eisenhower formed SHAEF. The Controlling Officer of Deception, in order to facilitate rapid and efficient working whilst retaining the general control of deception over the world (global deception as it came to be called!) and the general control of policy, was able to leave the more detailed planning to COSSAC, and later to Ops. B. SHAEF. He thus in fact confined himself to the exact task which had been originally allotted to him by the Chiefs of Staff. Consequently our traffic, whenever it touched on deception matters, was always submitted first to L.C.S., later to COSSAC, and still later to SHAEF for approval, as well as to the old established approving authorities. Consequently, too, the main deception plan for the invasion was worked out in detail by Ops. B. SHAEF with whom, as time went on, we dealt more and more closely.

We must turn to the actual work of the year, to the traffic, the plans and pieces of minor deception. Of the traffic—the questions asked and the answers given—no account need be given, partly because the Germans were thinking more and more defensively and were therefore more and more concerned with our measures of attack, still more because this side of the work was a permanent commitment, and has been sufficiently described and illustrated in the earlier years. But some mention must be made of some of the plans carried through by the agents.

Sabotage continued merrily. ZIGZAG started the year with his operation at the de Havilland works. Here on the night of 29 January camouflage experts made suitable arrangements for us, and aerial photographs gave a convincing picture of a considerable explosion. Reports from ZIGZAG and notices in the press seemed to convince the Germans of the success of the operation, the more so when news was sent to them that one of ZIGZAG's criminal assistants had been arrested for being in possession of gelignite and for suspicious behaviour in the neighbourhood of Hatfield. As the Germans were unwilling or unable to send a submarine for him, ZIGZAG was compelled to make his own arrangements for his getaway, and we contrived to have him shipped as a steward on board the *City of Lancaster*, which vessel he was to desert at Lisbon. He was carefully coached in his story and made to memorise a lengthy questionnaire dealing mainly with wireless stations at Nantes, Bordeaux, and Paris, and with German sabotage undertakings and methods.

Whilst the ship was at Lisbon ZIGZAG made contact with the Germans and eventually deserted as arranged; but there were moments of very great anxiety. We learned from secret sources that he was leaving on board pieces of coal given to him by the Germans and containing high explosive as a parting gift to the ship, and it was naturally impossible to be absolutely certain that ZIGZAG had not actually placed this coal in the bunkers, in order to set himself up with the Germans, without warning any of his former shipmates. An officer was hurried out to Lisbon, and it was discovered that ZIGZAG had given the coal into the charge of the captain and that the proposal had come in the first place from ZIGZAG himself.* He then returned into the charge of his German masters, and for the time disappeared from our ken.

The prospects opened up by his return to the enemy were impressive. He maintained himself that as a reward for his work he would be allowed to tour Germany and then take up a position in the Dienststelle at Paris, Nantes, or Angers; also, that he would certainly get another sabotage mission either to the United States, or perhaps, in charge of a large band of saboteurs to this country. He also believed that he could set up an organisation in France on fifth column lines, which would stay behind if the Germans evacuated France and which, of course, he would be able to hand over lock, stock, and barrel to the Allies. His own plan included the suggestion that he should undertake the assassination of Hitler as a one-man effort, but this proposal, with more than our customary caution, we declined to encourage. Perhaps we missed an opportunity, for ZIGZAG was an enterprising and practical criminal.

*ZIGZAG later received RM.10.000 for this bright idea.

Other sabotage was carried out in August by MUTT and JEFF. This was Plan BUNBURY, which consisted in arranging an explosion at a generating station at Bury St. Edmunds. After the target had been chosen, the Germans were communicated with and agreed to send sabotage equipment for the use of the agents. It must be remembered that the reputation of MUTT and JEFF, owing to the fluctuating demands of Norwegian deception, was always a little doubtful. Nonetheless the Germans believed in them sufficiently to supply the apparatus. In February of 1943 they had dropped a new transmitter and £200 by parachute for MUTT and JEFF in Aberdeenshire. At the end of May £400 and sabotage equipment were sent, but as the Germans dropped them in the wrong place MUTT and JEFF did not acknowledge receipt. Consequently, the Germans had to repeat the operation, when they dropped another £400, another radio set, and more sabotage equipment. The interesting fact about the equipment dropped was that the bulk of it was captured British material manufactured by SOE.

Plan BUNBURY, which was well written up and which produced a piece of flaming propaganda on a German broadcast claiming that over a hundred and fifty workmen had been killed, was a clear vindication of the principles for which sabotage was run. It maintained and confirmed the reputation of two agents who were important on the information as well as the sabotage side; it obtained for us samples of German sabotage equipment available to the Germans; it gave us knowledge of their sabotage technique; and, by the publicity resulting from the operation, it provided a security stimulus in factories and public utilities in this country.

Another successful plan which was completed in May was Plan MINCEMEAT. Shortly before the invasion of North Africa an aeroplane had crashed, a body had been washed ashore in Spain, and some fortunately unimportant papers had been shown to the Germans. It therefore appeared that a similar incident might be faked and turned to good account before some suitable major operation.

After consultation with Sir Bernard Spilsbury as to the medical possibilities, Mr. Bentley Purchase, the coroner, was consulted and asked to collect and retain an unclaimed body; the causes of death had to be not inconsistent with an aeroplane crash if a postmortem should be held. By the end of January 1943 Mr. Bentley Purchase had found a suitable body, which he retained on ice. It was decided to give the notional officer, who was given the name of Major Martin, the status of an officer in the Royal Marines, so that communications could be kept in naval hands and yet the officer wear a battle dress, as no normal uniform could be made to fit exactly.* Major Martin was then provided with a personality which was built up by a series of letters and other personal documents which he carried in his pocket. These were all written by appropriate persons and conveyed the picture of a youngish staff officer.

He was also given the official documentation of a major on the staff of the Chief of Combined Operations. The material document was a personal letter from Admiral Mountbatten to Admiral Cunningham, the naval C.-in-C. Mediterranean, to explain why Major Martin was travelling and carrying the main deception letter. This was a personal off-the-record letter from "Archie Nye" (V.C.I.G.S.) to "My dear Alex" (General Alexander). The intention of the letter was to cause the Germans to believe that Sicily was *not* the next target and that there were two operations being mounted in the Mediterranean. This was done by V.C.I.G.S. telling Alexander that he was taking the opportunity to send a personal letter by hand to give him an idea of the way the minds of members of the Chiefs of Staff Committee were running about the Mediterranean plans. A landing in Greece was indicated by mentioning that further troops and shipping had been allotted for the assaults on two main beaches. Attention was drawn away from Sicily by saying that General Wilson had wanted Sicily as his cover for the Greek operation, but for stated reasons the

---

*The difficulty of obtaining underclothes, owing to the system of coupon rationing, was overcome by the acceptance of a gift of thick underwear from the wardrobe of the late warden of New College, Oxford.

Chiefs of Staff felt that Alexander might be allowed to keep that as his cover target, as it was thought that the Germans would be more likely to deduce that Alexander's preparations were aimed at Sicily than were Wilson's; the Chiefs of Staff were suggesting that Wilson should choose something nearer the spot, such as the Dodecanese. That letter was dated 23 April.

In addition, to ensure that the papers were found even if the people who received the body did not go through Major Martin's pockets, he also carried a letter from Mountbatten to General Eisenhower, enclosing the proof of the pamphlet on joint operations to which Eisenhower was going to write a preface. This was sufficiently bulky to give an excuse for the three letters to be carried in a black government briefcase, which would give the Germans the greatest opportunity of laying hands on them.

It was decided to try and plant the body in Spain, where there would be close cooperation with the Germans and yet as much difficulty as possible for a thorough postmortem or careful investigations. Huelva was chosen as suitably near the route of aircraft flying to North Africa, and as being a place where the German consul was a highly efficient spy. Tides and local conditions were not unfavourable, and permission was obtained from the Admiralty to use a submarine *en route* to the Mediterranean. The Chiefs of Staff approved the material letter, and the Prime Minister's approval was also obtained. The letters were all typed, signed, and sealed as if they had been genuine, and Major Martin was dressed and placed, with the black briefcase, in a specially made container with some dry ice to delay decomposition. He was then driven up to the Clyde, where he was put on board H.M. Submarine *Seraph*. The container was labelled "Handle with Care, Optical Instruments for Special F.O.S. Shipment" (a fairly normal procedure), and the submarine's captain was given a suitable series of cover stories to provide for any eventualities in the launching of the body. The submarine sailed on 19 April. The final touch was the placing in Major Martin's pocket before he left of the dated counterfoil ticket stubs of two theatre tickets for the night of 22 April, so as to indicate that he had been in London too late to have left England and drifted ashore at Huelva unless he had travelled by air.

On 30 April the *Seraph* launched Major Martin from a position under a mile from the beach at Huelva, and also launched a capsized rubber dinghy from nearby. The body was found and taken over by the Spaniards. The British naval attaché in Madrid was instructed to make demarches to the Spanish Ministry of Marine to recover the papers. These started low and gradually increased in degree, as would be natural if we had discovered that a fairly uninteresting personality was in fact carrying important documents; at the same time they were kept on such a plane as (theoretically) not to arouse Spanish suspicions that we were really frightened that someone might get these documents, but in fact making it plain to them that we were so frightened.

The Spaniards succeeded in extracting the documents from the envelopes without breaking the seals, and the Spanish staff in Madrid, as we know from captured documents, supplied photographed copies of the papers to the Germans. These captured documents show that the Germans studied each phrase of the material letters with great care, and also were fully informed about the documentary build-up of Major Martin's personality; they also appreciated the point conveyed by the ticket counterfoils. They accepted the documents as absolutely genuine and promulgated the information, and their deductions, as being a hundred percent accurate, although they raised (but did not pursue) the question whether it was a plot.

Up till then O.K.W. appreciations had given Sicily as the next Mediterranean target, followed possibly by Sardinia and then Crete. From then on, not only were troops sent to the precise spot indicated in Greece, but all communications dealt with the impending Allied invasion of Greece, and in the western Mediterranean henceforward Sardinia was coupled at least level with Sicily. The Germans seem to have first of all taken Sardinia as the definite target, but worried whether there would be a diversionary assault on Sicily as well as an intelligence deception towards that area. Later they seem to have felt that Sicily would probably be assaulted as well. In any event, the German forces were well dispersed into the Greek area, and their reinforcements of Sardinia, from the time of MINCEMEAT on, more than kept pace (as they had not done before) with the reinforcements of Sicily. In addition, the minefields and other defences of Sicily, in as far as they were proceeded with, were much stronger at the northwestern or Sardinian end of the island than they were at the southeastern side, where the assault was in fact launched.

"Major Martin" received a fitting funeral with official representation. Probably that gallant but modest officer would have resented the appearance of his name in the official list of casualities almost as much as the tombstone which the curious can now visit at Huelva. Operation MINCEMEAT had nothing directly to do with the work of double agents, but it is properly described here because the plan originated in the minds of two members of the Twenty Committee and, as the Committee was the focal point of all information and misinformation which was allowed to go to the Germans, it was natural for it to discuss and further plans of this kind, especially at a time when deception control had hardly got fully into its stride. It was also essential to the scheme that it should be worked out by members of different services, and this made Twenty Committee machinery useful for the purpose.* At a larger stage

*This point is illustrated by an extract from the Twenty Committee minutes of 4 February 1943: "Plan MINCEMEAT. This plan is the same as Plan TROJAN HORSE. The details of the plan were put forward by Commander Montagu and F/Lt. Cholmondeley. It was reported that a body had been procured and it was explained that this would have to be used within three months, and that various points of detail would have to be decided before the Plan could be put into operation. The Plan was adopted by the Committee and it was agreed that copies of the Plan should be shown to the Directors of Intelligence; that the Air Ministry representatives on the Twenty Committee should make the necessary arrangements for the flight during which the body will be dropped; that Major Wingate (L.C.S.) should put the Plan before Colonel Bevan in order to obtain approval from the D.'s of P.; that the Admiralty representative should find out a suitable position off the Spanish coast where the body can be dropped; that the War Office representative should go into the question of providing the body with a name, necessary papers, etc. It was agreed that the N.A. Madrid should be informed of the Plan so that he will be able to cope with any unforeseen repercussions which may come his way." The plan of using a submarine came later.

the Controlling Officer of Deception sponsored the scheme, and in May took responsibility for the developments after the body had been washed ashore in Spain.

Other plans of the year can best be mentioned in connection with the development of the cases of individual agents. One of the main gains of the year was the return of TRICYCLE and the development of his body of associated agents. In America for various reasons TRICYCLE had not been wholly successful, but the strength of the case was always TRICYCLE's ability to impose himself and his views on the Germans when personal contact could be made. He was entirely confident that he could pacify the Germans if he visited Lisbon again, and his confidence proved to be well founded. He was at Lisbon for a week in October 1942, and apparently persuaded the Germans that his unsatisfactory work in America and his poor information were due to their failure to supply him with adequate funds. He succeeded in securing a considerable sum of money from them and new instructions, and returned to this country whence he communicated an increasing quantity of controlled information to them by secret ink. His linked agents BALLOON and GELATINE were still working, and in April METEOR arrived.

METEOR was a Yugoslav of good family, high character, and patriotic principles who had failed to escape from Yugoslavia when it was invaded. When trying to escape to Turkey he had got into touch with the Germans and had agreed to work for them as an anti-Bolshevist, but in no case against his own fellow countrymen. He was finally able to get out through the instrumentality of DREAD-NOUGHT. DREADNOUGHT was a daring and enterprising patriot who worked for a long time in the German service but, in fact, secured the escape of Yugoslavs and furthered other Allied ends. METEOR was to operate a new plan—in fact a plan of triple cross. He was to come to England, where he was to tell the British that he had been sent by the Germans. He was to hand over one cover address and explain his training in secret writing. Having told this story, he was expected by the Germans to continue working for them using in addition a different set of addresses and different inks. In fact, of course, he told us all, but he was very unwilling to undertake double-cross work since he wished to continue his career as a combatant officer. TRICYCLE helped us to persuade him of the importance of the double-cross work, and we therefore started through him a double correspondence with the Germans, METEOR's so-called controlled and uncontrolled letters.

TRICYCLE meantime was not content to remain in England passing other information, and plans were therefore made for him to visit Lisbon again in July. His cover for this visit was an ingenious one. He proposed to the Germans that he should open up an escape route for Yugoslav officers who had been interned in Switzerland. He contrived to get himself accepted by his own government for this purpose, and proposed to the Germans that they should use this method of introducing agents of their own into the party. He surmised, and rightly, that DREADNOUGHT would be used to help in the project. This "slipping-out" plan, as it was called, promised other advantages. It was hoped that some patriotic Yugoslavs whom the Germans would include in their "escapes" as cover would get to this country, that real German agents could be apprehended, and, furthermore, that TRICYCLE would be able to secure a wireless operator which would immensely increase his utility to us when he returned. In addition, TRICYCLE was most anxious to meet Johnny Jebson, or ARTIST as he came to be called, as he always believed that Jebson was ready and willing to sell out to this country.

Accordingly TRICYCLE spent a period from mid-July until mid-September at Lisbon, and successfully carried out the greater part of his scheme. He met ARTIST, who had indeed been collaborating with DREADNOUGHT, and he secured FREAK, another Yugoslav, who was passed out by the escape route after training in wireless and secret ink, and who arrived in England in December 1943. Thereafter FREAK acted as the wireless part of TRICYCLE's organisation. Another Yugoslav, THE WORM, had previously arrived after long delays in September, and was able to confirm the reports which he had had about DREADNOUGHT and ARTIST. TRI-CYCLE himself strengthened his own position by another visit to Lisbon in November which lasted until January. On this occasion he took better information to the Germans, and received instructions to pay FREAK and to give new instructions to GELATINE. Projects for improving the BALLOON channel were discussed but rejected. The Yugoslav ring, therefore, had become by the end of the year a highly important part of our organisation.

The second great acquisition of the year was BRUTUS, who had actually reached England in October 1942, but whose case was not accepted by the W. Board to whom the Twenty Committee presented it till January 1943. It was in all respects a complicated case, which, after an unprom-ising start, ultimately returned great dividends. BRUTUS was a Pole who had worked with great distinction as the head of a secret organisation in France in 1940 and 1941. He had been arrested by the Germans in November 1941 and kept in prison for eight and a half months, where he was treated at first with severity, but without brutality. He was "converted" by the Germans, as they thought, to the policy of collaboration with Germany and was allowed to "escape" in July 1942.

When he reached this country he told us the truth in all essentials, and himself strenuously urged that he should be used in what he called "the great game," i.e., to double-cross the enemy. He was expected to report military infor-mation of all kinds, but his primary task was to bring about collaboration between Polish military circles and the Ger-man army, and to create a Polish fifth column in England with possibilities of subversive propaganda and sabotage. Now BRUTUS was not only a man who had performed daring and distinguished work underground in France, but he was also a serving Polish officer. Three great difficulties therefore faced us.

The first was that his primary loyalty was to Poland, and that it would be necessary to inform the Poles here of what we were doing if he were used. Polish security was not such that we could indoctrinate the Poles completely in our proceedings, and difficulties of language made it a tricky business to watch the case for possible leakage. The second difficulty was even more ominous. We could after a time be sure of BRUTUS and his motives, but could we also be sure that the Germans really trusted him? They had indeed allowed him to reach this country, and had entrusted him with an important mission, but they knew how he had worked for the Allies in the early days, and it seemed to us possible or even probable that they might expect him, after he had been some time in this country and had seen the difficulties of collaboration between Poles and Germans, to revert to his former ideas and attach himself to the Allied cause once more. They had studied him from the psychological standpoint, and they must realise the cumulative effects of observing the war in England from a British standpoint, and might well feel that his loyalty to German interests might not be proof against British propaganda. If they convinced themselves that he had thrown them over, his traffic from this country would be a source of great danger to us.

The third difficulty which faced us was a political one. Russo-Polish tension was so great that the Foreign Office could not allow us to develop the political side of BRUTUS's work at all for fear of awkward repercussions. This fact was a sort of millstone round the neck of the case, and prevented us from building up the network of subagents which the Germans wanted and which would have made the case of even greater importance and value than it was. Nevertheless it was decided to run the case "for a time at any rate," and to inform the Poles, who agreed that they should not see copies of the traffic; but it was also determined by the W. Board that so far as possible the case should not be used for operational deception. In the event the position of BRUTUS was such that he was the best placed of all our agents for sending over military information; and, consequently, as confidence grew both in him and in the Germans'

belief in him, he was used more and more and took a large
part in the deception for OVERLORD. In June BRUTUS was
in trouble with his own countrymen as he took part in
political activities against the head of the Polish air force
and was involved in court-martial proceedings. This threatened the extinction of the case; but the difficulty was overcome, and BRUTUS continued to serve in a variety of military
appointments. He was thus admirably placed for the transmission of military information.

The GARBO case went on from strength to strength during
the year. The one-man band of Lisbon developed into an
orchestra, and an orchestra which played a more and more
ambitious programme. GARBO himself turned out to be
something of a genius. He was the master of a facile and
lurid style in writing; he showed great industry and ingenuity coupled with a passionate and quixotic zeal for his
task. Throughout the year he worked on an average six to
eight hours a day drafting secret letters, encyphering, com-
posing cover texts, and planning for the future. Moreover,
in March he began to operate a wireless set, the purchase
of which was arranged through his agent No. 4, who also
recruited an amateur operator (featured as a Communist
and supposed to be working for people whom he believed
to be Spanish Reds). In fact, of course, he was one of our
own operators. The Germans showed their trust by sending
over for him the identical cypher then in use between certain
German Secret Service stations. When later they changed,
they entrusted GARBO with a new cypher based on the one
newly introduced.

The number of subagents was increased and the flood of
correspondence continued in addition to the wireless messages. By August 1944 (if for a moment we might anticipate
events) the Germans had received some four hundred secret
letters and about two thousand long wireless messages from
the organisation, and had supplied GARBO with some
£20,000. During 1943 GARBO was used to pass over the
greater part of Plan STARKEY, and had also described to the
Germans the extensions of a great underground depot for

small arms and a complete system of underground communications centring in the Chislehurst caves. It was thought that this depot might well serve in a cover plan for an invasion from the southeast coast.

By the spring of 1944 GARBO was the chief of an organisation comprising fourteen active agents and eleven well-placed contacts, especially one at the Ministry of Information, all, with the exception of GARBO himself, being in fact notional, though fully trusted by the Germans. He had also furnished himself with a deputy and a substitute wireless operator, and had established his principal assistants at Glasgow, Methil, Harwich, Dover, Brighton, Exeter, and Swansea.

Other recruits of 1943 included FIDO, who arrived in July, a French air force pilot whose primary mission was to steal an aeroplane in this country and fly back to the Germans. In addition he was to send information on aviation, concentration of troops and aircraft, and technical matters. He could write secret letters but had no method of receiving messages or instructions. In August TREASURE arrived, a French citizen of Russian origin. TREASURE was an intelligent but temperamental woman who was controlled by Kliemann of I. Luft, Paris, who also controlled DRAGON-FLY. She communicated by secret writing, but could receive instructions by wireless, and at a later date she succeeded in obtaining a wireless transmitter herself.

BEETLE landed in Iceland with a wireless set and a barometer as previously mentioned in chapter 9, and in November SNIPER a pilot in the Belgian air force, was introduced to this country through Spain. SNIPER was an agent of I.T/LW Brussels and had important questions to answer in connection with scientific apparatus and aircraft matters, and, most important of all, methods used in antisubmarine warfare. He received by w/t and was to be sent a transmitting set later. Meantime he could communicate by secret writing. At a later date, when he was to return to Belgium, a transmitting set was buried for him at Turnhout.

There were losses as well as gains. CARELESS, whose

personal conduct had compelled us to imprison him, turned truculent and had to be crossed off in January, and FATHER, whose position was embarassing owing to the high grade of the questions asked him and the impossibility of providing safe but plausible answers, had to be given an overseas posting in June. WATCHDOG was closed down in Canada in the summer and DRAGONFLY petered out owing to the inability of the Germans to pay him at the end of the year.

At the end of 1943, then, the double agent system was in appearance far more powerful and better equipped than it had ever been before. There was a far more than adequate supply of agents communicating by wireless, by secret ink, and at need by personal contact; and there was ample evidence that the Germans had confidence in their agents. But appearances are often deceptive; it was pointed out at the beginning of the chapter that the double-cross system was always in danger, and as will be shown in the next chapter, we were not very far from failure just before the period of our greatest success.

11: DECEPTION TO COVER THE NORMANDY LANDINGS AND THE INVASION OF FRANCE

From the beginning of 1944 all our activities were swallowed up in the one absorbing interest of the grand strategic deception for the Normandy invasion. The climax which we had hoped for from the beginning was approaching and all other aspects of the work sank into insignificance—at least for the time. It will be remembered that we had always expected that at some one moment all the agents would be recklessly and gladly blown sky high in carrying out the grand deception, and that this one great coup would both repay us many times over for all the efforts of the previous years and bring our work to an end. When exactly the day would be we could not of course tell, but at the end of 1943 it was obviously drawing near. Counterespionage activities, appreciations of the enemy's intentions as mirrored in the traffic, small *ad hoc* deceptions, domestic details connected with the agents, the "vetting" of new cases and the proving and testing of old ones—all these things went on, but they seemed of little account compared with the preparation of the deception which was to cover the landings and the invasion.

It was considered by the planners of Operation NEPTUNE (the naval portion of OVERLORD) that its hazards depended largely upon the success or failure of a cover plan; but in the nature of things this plan could only work within narrow limits. This had not been the case in earlier enterprises. There had been a time when the Germans had been uncertain whether an attack would come in northwest Africa or in the Mediterranean, and again when they had had to envisage the possibilities of being invaded in the "soft under-belly," or in the Bay of Biscay, or in Norway and Denmark.

Possibly vulnerable areas had been numerous and widely divided from one another. But by the early spring of 1944 it was utterly impossible to disguise the fact that the major attack would come somewhere between the Cherbourg peninsula and Dunkirk; the true preparations which could not be wholly disguised indicated this beyond all doubt, and the distance from the base at which fighter cover could be supplied helped to define the limits. The deception policy was dictated by these circumstances, and therefore of necessity it boiled down to a simple policy of three points: first to postpone the date of attack, secondly to indicate that the attack would come in the east rather than in the west of the threatened area, and thirdly, after the real attack had taken place, to suggest that it was only a first blow and that a second and even weightier assault would follow in the Pas de Calais area, i.e., at the eastern end of the target.

Manifestly then the chief task of the agents would be to build up the forces which threatened this area, and this would be a long-distance task. Speculations, guesses, or leakages, would have little or no effect on the German military mind, for the German staff officer would make his own appreciations and his own guesses from the facts put before him. What he would require would be facts, and the facts which the agents could supply would include the location and identification of formations, units, headquarters, assembly areas and the like. This was precisely the task which the agents had been trained and built up to perform, and if results are any criterion they did it very well.

Since this is a history of the work of double agents, the deception plan is here viewed and discussed only from the side of the double-cross agents, but it is necessary at this stage to state the obvious fact, which, though obvious, might otherwise be overlooked, that double-cross agents were only a part of the machinery of deception which was used. The cover plan was fixed in the Germans' mind by wireless deception (the Y Service), by visual deception (e.g., dummy assault craft) by the actual movement of troops in this country, by regulations and bans on various parts of the coast, and so forth. It is otiose to consider which part of the plan contributed most to the ultimate success—and indeed such an assessment, if worth while, could only be made by those in charge of the whole deception. For our purpose it is sufficient to state that the special agents were one of the channels by which the deception plan was passed over to the enemy, and that so far as can be ascertained, our particular part of the plan was well and truly carried out. Whether the agents served best to support the bogus wireless signals (the Y Service) which were put on the air to confirm the existence of notional divisions, or whether the Y Service served rather to support the reports of the agents, is an idle and unprofitable speculation. What we can be sure of is that the agents did justify the trust reposed in them and in the double-cross system.

It was not proposed to use all the agents in this great affair, for in it all risk of error had to be avoided where avoidance was possible. In our everyday business it was not fatal if any one agent blundered or became suspect, but in this matter any real mistake might be fatal. An agent who, in spite of all precautions on our part, turned out not to be believed by the enemy, might wreck the whole enterprise, or, even worse, his messages might be "read in reverse" and the true target of attack be exposed instead of concealed by him. So much did those in charge of deception feel the force of this argument that they were for a time in favour of cutting down the agents to the barest minimum in order to use only the safest channels—indeed at one time they suggested the elimination of all except the GARBO network. This suggestion we successfully resisted. We pointed out that even the apparently most trusted agent might suddenly collapse for reasons outside our control (as indeed happened shortly afterwards in the case of TRICYCLE); that agents' reports were often not graded before being passed on by the Germans; and that even quite humble members of the team might contribute—either by giving the Germans confirmation of details or even only by confusing them with a mass of material. By mutual agreement, however, it was settled that only the best agents should transmit definite deception material, but that the rest should be kept going for subsidiary purposes.

Little has been said previously in this narrative about the degree of trust reposed in the individual agents, but here it must be emphasised that we were continuously assessing and reassessing their reputation with the enemy. This was done in a variety of ways: by a most careful scrutiny of all the questions asked, by watching the payments made (a very good, if rough, test of an agent's value), by remarks made at interviews in cases where our agents had personal contact, and by intelligence information of various kinds. All this revealed with fair accuracy how the agents were regarded on the other side, and it was clear that in many cases their reputation varied greatly with the course of events. Thus MUTT and JEFF appeared to us and to their case officer to be sometimes on the crest of the wave and considered as valuable sources of information as well as lucky though not very highly skilled saboteurs, at other times to be looked upon with the gravest suspicion. In the early months of 1944 secret sources indicated clearly that GARBO and TRICYCLE were the most highly thought of, but their relative value oscillated, probably according not only to the information they gave, but also according to the claims made for them by their own spy-masters. This study of form and day-to-day appraisement of all members of the team was an absorbingly interesting as well as a vitally necessary task.

At the turn of the year the W. Board reviewed the cases in the light of the information furnished by us. We were able to show that in most cases there was just cause for confidence, and accordingly in December the TRICYCLE group was passed fit for use in strategic deception. In January, after considerable hesitation, it was decided that BRUTUS should be used for the same purpose, since secret sources revealed that our fears of German mistrust in him were not justified. The main agents, therefore, to be used were GARBO, TRICYCLE (fortified by the FREAK transmissions), and BRUTUS. Others who would be used to assist included TREASURE, TATE, MULLET, GELATINE, BRONX, possibly MUTT and JEFF, and others of less importance. It seemed, therefore, that though it had been long in coming, the climax found us well prepared and more than adequately staffed.

But here we must revert to the concluding paragraph of the last chapter, where it was stated that though success came, failure was dangerously close. In fact, for six reasons the whole existence of the double-cross system hung in the balance just before D Day. Let us summarise these reasons.

1. In the first place knowledge of double-cross work had been, owing to the length of the war and its almost infinite complications and developments, disseminated to a dangerous extent. Two agents were operating in Iceland, a GARBO subagent was active in Canada, and another had gone to Ceylon. Moreover, a considerable and highly successful double-cross system, which unfortunately cannot be described here, had been run in the Middle East. All these commitments meant that a great number of persons had to be informed of the theory and practice of double-cross activities. Furthermore, it had been realised that when the Germans were driven out of occupied territory they would leave everywhere a "stay-behind"organisation of agents trained to carry on espionage and to make reports to Germany, and it was expected that with reasonably good fortune we should be able to apprehend many of them and use some of them as double-cross agents. If they were to be thus used it was imperative that they should be taken over at once by officers, whether British or American, prepared to operate them, and consequently a large number of officers had to be trained in this special work. In fact in the later stages of the war B.1.A had to set up something in the nature of a school for education in double-cross.

In the early days knowledge of double-cross work had been confined to a small esoteric ring of persons; by 1944 it was widely spread in ever-expanding circles.* However careful individuals may be (and admitting also the argument to which many would subscribe that junior officers are usually more "secure" than their seniors!), it is impossible to avoid the conclusion that there must sooner or later be leakage when a secret is shared by a great number of people. If leakage occurred, then in time knowledge would seep through to the enemy. Some of the officers who had been taught would, for example, fall into enemy hands. And, to carry the argument one step further, if the Germans ever became alive to the fact that we were working a double-cross system on a large scale, they would certainly suspect all the agents, and our period of usefulness would then be at an end.

2. The second danger came through just such an instance of leakage. Late in 1943 certain Germans, including one Erich Carl, a member of the German War Graves Commission in the Low Countries and probably an Abwehr agent, was repatriated to Germany. From an informer we learned that thirty-three persons, including Carl, had been for some time interned in the Isle of Man, and that whilst there a secret system of signalling between their camp and Camp WX, which contained persons who had been at Ham, had been developed. An investigation by M.I.5 officers was undertaken at Dartmoor in December 1943, since the more important prisoners of Camp WX had been moved there, and a report on the investigation established beyond doubt the seriousness of the situation. It appeared almost certain that an account of the case of JEFF (who was an inmate of Camp WX) had reached Germany and highly likely that TATE's case was also compromised. About subsequent developments in Germany there is no certainty. Probably the reports of those repatriated, if they ever reached those in authority, were only partially believed, and in fact no serious

*In February 1941 D.M.I. had insisted that knowledge of the work should be confined to the smallest possible number of persons. For security reasons he had even objected to the use of the words "XX agent" in an aide-memoire prepared by B.1.A for his own personal persual!

repercussions were observed by us. None the less the incident was alarming, and clearly we had only escaped a disaster by a narrow margin.

3. Another danger came from a different angle. We had satisfied ourselves that we did in fact control the German system in England and that there were no competitors in this country. In the autumn of 1943, however, we became aware that certain Germans in the Peninsula, notably OSTRO, were in fact giving information to the Germans which, as they declared, came from their agents in England. In fact these agents were notional, and their reports were constructed from rumour aided by invention and surmise. To us, however, they seemed in the highest degree dangerous. Not only was it possible that OSTRO reports would gain more credence in Berlin than the reports of our own agents, but also it was not impossible that OSTRO might by a fluke give the exact area of attack on the Continent, and thus destroy the deception plan. Against this it was argued by some that false reports of this kind might well do us more good than harm, since their inaccuracy would confuse the enemy and cause him to dissipate his efforts. On balance, however, the Twenty Committee were strongly of the opinion that the danger predominated, and a variety of schemes was put forward for the elimination of OSTRO. They did not succeed. Consequently OSTRO continued to operate and cause us anxiety till the end of the war.

4. A fourth danger came from internal changes in the German service. The inefficiency of the Abwehr and complaints about its political unreliability led to the dismissal of its head, Admiral Canaris, in February 1944. The future of the organisation was then discussed at a series of conferences, and a negotiated settlement was reached in May. This was announced by Himmler at a general Abwehr conference at Salzburg. By this settlement, though the Abwehr was abolished, the O.K.W. retained some powers in the newly formed Mil. Amt, and the former Abwehr directors remained at the head of the Mil. Amt. After the attempt

on Hitler's life of 20 July in which many former Abwehr
officers were implicated, the Mil. Amt became part of Amt
VI of the Reichssicherheitshauptamt (R.S.H.A.). The details of the changes do not matter, but the collapse of the
Abwehr, with which as well as against which we had learned
to work, was a blow to us. If the changes had been made
earlier it is probable that the new brooms would have swept
away much which we were concerned to preserve. Once
again, the margin of safety for our double-cross system was
very small.

5. A more subtle danger, and one which threatened to
destroy all our plans, lay in the tendency of Abwehr officials
to desert the sinking ship. Shrewd observers among the
Germans decided early on which side victory would ultimately lie and made their plans accordingly. Some, such
as JUNIOR, who was brought over to us in November 1943
after earlier attempts to join us, had always been anti-Nazi;
others tried to come for purely selfish motives. At the beginning of 1944 this was excessively dangerous for us. If such
an Abwehr agent changed sides and joined the British, he
would quite certainly tell us of all the German agents he
knew operating in England, and these would in fact be our
own controlled agents. Unfortunately the Germans would
know that the traitor could and would give away all this
information, and consequently they would expect the arrest
of GARBO, TRICYCLE, BRUTUS, TATE, and the rest. If the
agents continued to work as if nothing had happened the
Germans would assume that they were under our control.
In short, the German turncoat, trying to assist us, would
in fact destroy our entire system. In this case again we just
and only just survived long enough, but it is difficult to
avoid the conclusion that a few more months of delay in
invasion would have ended our activities.

6. Finally there came a major disaster just before D Day,
a disaster not unconnected with the danger explained in
the paragraph above. It will be remembered that TRICYCLE
had visited Lisbon in the summer and autumn of 1943 in

order to arrange his "slipping-out" plan, and that there he obtained a great deal of information from ARTIST. TRICYCLE reported on his return that he was "absolutely sure" that ARTIST knew that he was working for the British. He also reported that ARTIST was in fear of the Gestapo, against whom the Abwehr protected him with difficulty, and that ARTIST had discussed the possibility of himself contriving to get to England. In later months the position of ARTIST clarified itself, and by the end of September he had agreed to participate actively with us in order to further his professed anti-Nazi views.

ARTIST gave us much useful information, but some of it was highly embarrassing, in particular details which would have made it possible for us to capture GARBO, had we not already controlled him. The same reason—i.e. the desire to maintain our system intact and avoid unfortunate revelations—caused us to evacuate JUNIOR clandestinely in November. TRICYCLE returned to Lisbon in that same month, and stayed till January, and on this occasion British representatives also went over and had discussions with ARTIST. They formed the opinion that ARTIST was governed by a genuine dislike of Naziism, by a conviction that Germany had lost the war, by fear of communism, by a contempt for the inefficiency and corruption of the Abwehr, and by the realisation that it was high time to insure his own business future for the postwar world.

In February TRICYCLE went once more to Lisbon carrying information so good that it was expected to confirm the high position which he held in Abwehr regard. He returned in April. The case therefore seemed to stand well as D Day approached, but the position was in reality a perilous one, for we had placed far too much reliance on ARTIST, and still more on ARTIST's own judgment of his position vis-a-vis the various German services. The obtaining of evidence of enemy intentions and methods is a legitimate and important function of double-cross work, and ARTIST could be exceptionally valuable not only in telling us about the Abwehr but also, as we hoped, in obtaining information about rocket guns and similar weapons. But the plain truth is that in the spring of 1944 deception was of overriding importance, and that its security was jeopardised by ARTIST's peculiar position. He was in fact a double-cross agent living on the Continent, and whatever his motives and however strong his attachment to us, he was in a position to betray us if he wished.

We had stopped all seamen agents from going to the Peninsula, lest they should unwittingly give away information, but we left ARTIST (however unlikely treachery on his part might be) in a position where he might betray or be forced into disclosures. Yet what else could we have done? If we evacuated ARTIST and continued to use our agents, then we ran the risk explained above—i.e., that the Germans would realise that all the agents were controlled. So strongly did GARBO's case officer feel the force of these arguments that he recommended at the end of February that GARBO should not be used for deception in case, halfway through the plan, ARTIST should cause it to collapse.

The blow fell early in May, when we learned that ARTIST had been tricked into leaving Portugal and had been conveyed to Germany. It was hoped, and there was some evidence to support the theory, that he had become suspect only because of his financial dealings, but that belief was small consolation. Under interrogation it was to be presumed that much, if not all, of the history of his activities would come to light, and in that case many of our best cases were doomed. The TRICYCLE case, including the use of the FREAK transmitter, had to be brought to an end.

On the most optimistic estimate, therefore, we had lost one of the most important cases, or sets of cases, just as D Day approached; on the most pessimistic, the whole deception through double-cross agents was in danger. Once more, however, we were saved by time and fortune. D Day arrived before the Germans had succeeded in unravelling all the tangled skein of the ARTIST case, and presumably there was little opportunity after D Day for patient research into such matters in German offices.

The summary above should suffice to show the narrowness of the margin by which our system won through, but in spite of all these dangers it did hold long enough not only to perform its task in the grand deception plan, but even to be of great service in the period after the plan had succeeded. To the grand deception plan we must now revert.

The agents who remained proved amply sufficient to carry out our assignment after the assistance of the TRICYCLE group was lost, but a heavier burden had to be carried by BRUTUS than had at first been contemplated. It will be remembered that the essence of the plan was the threat to the Pas de Calais area, and that this threat was based upon the creation of certain notional forces, mainly in southeast England—or, to be more exact, the creation of the belief in the existence and location of these forces in the German mind. The method used, so far as double-cross agents were concerned, was the building up of a false British order of battle for the Germans, a method which had previously been used with the greatest success in the Middle East.

Previous attempts of the same nature in England had met with difficulties. Already in February 1943, acting on a general directive from L.C.S., Home Forces had begun to construct a false order of battle; in March, after a correct order had been obtained, it was agreed that it might be possible to create seven to ten bogus divisions in this country. But the Twenty Committee, and particularly the representatives of Home Forces there, were of opinion that the agents could only "create" these divisions if they were backed up by necessary w/t traffic. Here considerations of manpower were the decisive factor, and after consultations between L.C.S., the chief signals officer and Sigs. 2 of the War Office, it became more and more evident that shortage of manpower made adequate w/t support impracticable. In June, after discussion with COSSAC and the War Office, L.C.S. reported that w/t deception was for the time being impossible. It was not, therefore, until the winter of 1943 to 1944 that the creation of the false order of battle really got into its stride, for by that time w/t cover was available and able to play a decisive part.

The plan, in broad outline, was to create two army groups, one real (Twenty-first Army Group) and one notional (First United States Army Group or FUSAG). When the Twenty-first Army Group went overseas, FUSAG would be left consisting of the U.S. Third Army (real) and the British Fourth Army (notional). In the final stage, when the U.S. Third Army had gone overseas, on about D + 30, FUSAG would be left with only notional formations, these being eventually the Fourteenth U.S. Army and the Fourth British Army. In the early stages before D Day the map for the real order of battle showed the main weight of our forces in the Midlands, the west and the southwest; the false order of battle showed the main weight in Scotland, the east and the southeast.

Once the false order of battle was firmly fixed in the German mind and the German files, the deduction on their part that the assault must come in the Pas de Calais area was inevitable, and there is abundant evidence that the Germans did in fact swallow the deception plan hook, line, and sinker. A German map of the British order of battle as on 15 May 1944 which was later captured in Italy showed how completely our imaginary order of battle had been accepted and was largely based on the information supplied by the double-cross agents, especially GARBO and BRUTUS. A recognition booklet captured in France, which had been issued to field commanders, included coloured drawings of our notional divisional signs. The deduction mentioned above, which was the kernel of the whole plan, was stated with precision by the Japanese M.A. Berlin on 9 June to Tokyo and to the Japanese M.A.s in Istanbul, Sofia, Madrid, and Lisbon. A part of his message ran thus " . . . but because one separate Army Group is stationed on the southeast coast of Britain, it is expected that plans will be made for this to land in the Calais and Dunkirk areas."

D Day was 6 June, but the message above shows that the deception plan was not completed with the successful and unexpected landing. On D + 3 GARBO, after a conference with all his agents, sent over a full report which he requested might be submitted urgently to the German High Command. In this he set out in concentrated form the order of battle in this country, claimed that seventy-five divisions (instead of about fifty) existed at D Day, pointed out that no FUSAG formation was taking part in the attack, and deduced that the real operation was only a diversionary attack shortly to be followed by an assault in the Pas de Calais area.

Reactions to this information were soon observed. Paris reported to Madrid that Rundstedt regarded an item of information about the Guards Armoured Division as especially important and that, like Oliver Twist, he had "asked for more." The head of the German Secret Service in Berlin told Madrid that Himmler had expressed appreciation of the work carried out by the GARBO organisation and that further efforts must be made to ascertain in good time the destination of the troops in the southeast of England.* Finally, on 11 June (D + 5) an appreciation was sent by Berlin to Madrid stating that "all reports received in the last week from Arabel (GARBO) undertaking have been confirmed without exception and are to be described as especially valuable."

It appears indeed that the Germans believed to the end of the chapter that the Pas de Calais attack was intended and would have been delivered if the Normandy attack had not been more successful than had been expected. Evidence of the movements of German troops entirely supports this view. Thus immediately after the receipt of the message of 9 June the 116th Panzer Division, which had been stationed northwest of Paris, was ordered to move to the Somme, and the First S.S. Panzer Division was moved from Turnhout to

---

*On 18 October the *Times* published an account by its military correspondent of a record of telephone conversations of senior German commanders and staff officers, covering the months of June and July, which had fallen into our hands. From this it appears that on 9 June the Seventh German Army asked for reinforcements. The account continues: "Rommel's reply revealed how completely the Germans had been bluffed. He could not (he said) share the anxiety of the Seventh Army about Cherbourg because O.H.L. (German Supreme Command) expected a big landing higher up the coast in the course of the next few days."

Ghent—i.e., both converged on the Pas de Calais. Similarly, the Eighty-fifth Infantry Division stationed north of the Somme, and which had received orders to move (presumably towards the beachhead) had its orders cancelled and was recalled. In all some seven offensive German divisions which were expected to be sent to the Cherbourg area were retained in the Pas de Calais area for a fortnight after D Day. It was the opinion of Jodl, if any credence is to be given to newspaper reports, that fifteen divisions had been held in the Pas de Calais area to counter any landing there and to protect V weapon sites, and that this had been a fatal strategic error on the part of the German command.

The elegance of the deception plan should now be apparent. It not only deceived the Germans as to the main assault, but maintained the threat after the real assault had taken place. And more than this. Each successive step served to confirm the truth of the whole cover plan. Thus when the troops of the real formations reached France, they were always troops who had been identified and reported upon by the agents. In consequence the Germans, finding these reports which they could check from prisoners accurate, were disposed to believe with equal confidence in the rest of the reports which concerned the troops, real and notional, still in England. Thus, in German eyes, the threat to the Pas de Calais was as great and dangerous in July as it had been in May. In fact, and beyond the wildest hopes of those responsible, the threat held until the autumn, and it was not until 25 October that the Japanese M.A. in Stockholm reported to Tokyo that FUSAG had been broken up.

Here it must be repeated that it is not the purpose of this narrative to tell the history of deception except in the broadest outline and only in so far as is necessary to explain the work of double-cross agents. The double-cross system was only a channel by which those controlling deception passed their plans to the enemy. The credit for the success as well as for the plans themselves belongs entirely to "deception": the merit of the double-cross system lies in the fact that the agents proved themselves to be a safe and highly efficient channel, or, in other words, an instrument which deception was able to use effectively. It must not be forgotten, also, that the messages sent by the chief agents with regard to the order of battle is not the whole of the double-cross story, for the double-cross system contributed in other ways as well to the success of the deception. The point needs illustration.

In the first place, when participating in the deception for OVERLORD we reaped the full advantage of having the German intelligence service here under our control, because we felt confident by that time that our agents had no competitors in this country. In consequence of this we were able to state with confidence what the Germans did *not* know about our preparations as well as what they did know. The absence of detailed questions about the pipelines and about "Mulberries" indicated that German knowledge of such things as these was small or nonexistent. In other words, once more as in the days of TORCH, the actual denial of information to the enemy (which we could guarantee) was as important as the handing to the enemy of misinformation. OVERLORD, viewed in this light, owed a great debt not only to deception but also to security.

Secondly, mention must be made of an ingenious and somewhat elaborate plan designed to draw the attention of the Germans to the Pas de Calais area at an early date and by a method unconnected with the ordinary troop identifications and movements. This plan was known as Plan PREMIUM, and was worked through MULLET, who, in collusion with PUPPET, sent in reports to HAMLET for transmission to Brussels. MULLET in his earlier life had filled a not inconspicuous position in the insurance world in Belgium; he was now notionally moved into one of the largest insurance companies here. Thence he sent a series of interesting reports on his work to the Germans. In essence, the burden of these was that his company had in peacetime (as was true) carried out a great deal of insurance work for companies and factories in the Low Countries and in north-

ern France, and was in consequence in possession of a mass
of industrial and economic information with regard to these
districts. The government had requested the company to
provide this material, insofar as it dealt with the Pas de
Calais area, in a suitable form for unspecified government
purposes; and MULLET had been put in charge of the
collection and arrangement of the data. Later evidence
indicates that HAMLET himself ceased to work for the Brussels Stelle in April 1944, though he parted on good terms
from his employers, and it is not known whether or not the
pointer towards the Pas de Calais given by MULLET was
in fact effective. In any case the attempt to add evidence
of the point threatened was well worth making.

Thirdly, a part of the cover plan was implemented by
TATE. It will be remembered that in 1941 TATE had been
notionally established on his friend's farm at Radlett and
had thus escaped military service. Agricultural work had
kept him tied, except for occasional weekends which he
spent in London, and consequently he had been enabled
to get sufficient, but not too much, information for the
Germans. With an eye on the future we had invented for
him a friend of his employer's who lived near Wye in Kent
and who was also a farmer. To this friend TATE used sometimes to go to assist in agricultural operations, usually at
times when it seemed desirable to us that reliable military
information should be passed to the Germans from that
part of the country.

Accordingly, towards the end of May TATE paid one of
his visits to Wye, and, since the Germans had urged him in
April to exert every effort to find out about invasion preparations, he even took the risk of moving his transmitter
there. TATE, as we had built him up in the Germans' minds,
had something of a genius for making friends; it was not,
therefore, surprising that he became acquainted with a railway clerk from Ashford. From this man he procured and
sent on to Germany all the railway arrangements for moving
the FUSAG forces from their concentration areas to the em-
barkation ports, thus reinforcing from a new angle the
imminence of the threat to the Pas de Calais. TATE's re-

ports from Wye were so much appreciated that one Abwehr official, as we learned subsequently, was of opinion that they could "even decide the outcome of the war."

Finally, in considering the work of the agents in the deception plan, it should be remembered that some contributed indirectly not only by what they reported, but by what they did not. Thus TREASURE, who was accustomed to pass the weekends at Bristol, was able to say that she observed hardly any troop movements in southwest England, and thus assisted to confirm the Germans' belief that the weight of the blow would come from the southeast.

The letter-writing agents also played a part, especially BRONX. The Germans believed in the ability of BRONX to pick up any indication of the immediate objective of the invasion which was to be had in London; but they realised, of course, that a warning from her by letter would reach them too late. Consequently at the beginning of March they sent her a code, of which the substance was that she should telegraph to Lisbon for sums of varying amounts which she needed for her dentist. The sums would show whether invasion was likely to come in northern France, in the Bay of Biscay, in the Mediterranean, in Denmark, in Norway, or in the Balkans. BRONX in a secret letter improved this code by introducing a doctor and a physician as well as the dentist in order to show how far she could guarantee the credibility of her message, and also arranged to indicate the estimated date of the invasion.

It was part of the deception plan to retain German forces, especially a Panzer division, in the Bordeaux area and prevent them from being hurried to the real area of the invasion. This part of the plan could not hold for long, but it might be of great advantage if the Germans could be persuaded even for a short time that there was danger of landings in the Bordeaux district. Consequently on 15 May BRONX wired to her Lisbon bank "Envoyez vite cinquante livres. J'ai besoin pour mon dentiste." The interpretation of this code telegram was: "I have definite news that a landing will be made in the Bay of Biscay in about one month—i.e., about 15 June." BRONX then explained by letter that she had got her information from a slightly intoxicated officer friend, who had been told that an airborne attack on Bordeaux was to take place that day. Next day he had implored her to keep quiet, as the attack had been postponed for a month, i.e., until about 15 June.

It may well seem that this action of BRONX's was too fantastic to be likely to have any effect; but two pieces of evidence suggest that it may have been not wholly wasted. In the first place, when invasion took place, the Panzer division *was* kept in the Bordeaux area and not pushed north at once towards Cherbourg. The second piece of evidence is more interesting. Many months later in March 1945, when the Germans were expecting new attacks, they wrote a letter to BRONX and asked her to telegraph again to tell them where to expect the next blow. Their message runs as follows: "When we should expect a new invasion, either by landing or by parachute, let us know in the following code. Send. I need for my dentist . . . . Landing south of Sweden £30, landing in Norway £40, Landing in Denmark £50, landing in the German Bay £60, landing and parachuting in the German Bay £70. Parachuting to the west of Berlin £80. Parachuting to the west of Berlin and landing in the German Bay £100." It is difficult to believe that the Germans would have used this same code again, nearly a year later, if they had been dissatisfied with its use by BRONX in May of 1944.

In concluding this chapter on the use of double-cross agents in the great strategic deception of 1944, it should be mentioned once more that the agents were only one of the channels through which the deception was carried out. How effective they were in comparison with other channels and other instruments matters very little and could only be decided after the evidence from the German side has been received and sorted out and after the history of deception has been written. But even at this stage we should not be guilty of hubris if we claimed that the double-cross system did what was demanded of it with efficiency and success. Writing on 25 October 1944 to the Director General Security Service, the Controlling Officer of Deception said:

Some days ago the Chiefs of Staff made some very complimentary remarks regarding the success which had attended deception plans in the last few years. Though it is very pleasant to receive such praise, I am fully alive to the fact that nothing could have been accomplished without the help and cooperation of various ministries and departments. In this connection the contribution towards the success of deception plans which has been made by M.I.5 has been outstanding. B.1.A and the Twenty Committee have from the earliest days gone out of their way to help, and when the history of this war is written, I believe it will be found that the German High Command was, largely through the medium of B.1.A channels, induced to make faulty dispositions, in particular during the vital post-OVERLORD D Day period. The future can alone confirm or disprove this contention.

12: USE OF THE SYSTEM IN THE LAST YEAR OF THE WAR

A considerable body of opinion in the summer of 1944 supported the view that the double-cross system had fulfilled its function and exhausted its usefulness, and that it might in consequence be dissolved. There was much to be said for this view. It had always been thought that the grand deception would blow all the agents and that, once the Germans had realised the manner in which they had been tricked, it was better to abolish the whole system and deny them all information whatever. It was further pointed out that there were practical difficulties in continuing the cases; SHAEF could provide a stream of traffic so long as there was a deception to be put over, but it was not easy to keep the stream running after the invasion had taken place and it would probably be a waste of time to continue to bolster up the stories of the notional divisions. Still more, considerations of manpower obtruded themselves. B.1.A had trained a great many officers for service overseas; but since some B.1.A officers, and especially wireless experts, must themselves go across to run double-cross cases in Europe, it was apparent that there would be a shortage of those competent to deal with old and new cases in this country.

Furthermore, it was urged that the centre of gravity had shifted, that agents in this country were a back number, and that the general interest was better served by concentrating upon those "stay-behind" agents left by the Germans as they retreated rather than upon the rump of agents left in Great Britain. Many of their "stay-behind" agents would undoubtedly fall into our hands. It is hard enough to conceal a wireless transmitting set in an ordered community and in conditions where a great part of the rule of law still prevails; in districts which had just passed from the control of one power to that of another it would be next-door to impossible. Spy-fever would be rife; everyone would suspect his neighbour; most people would be anxious to ingratiate themselves with the conquerors; hardly any excuse would be needed to search rooms or houses of anyone or where the slightest suspicion rested; there would be no privacy and no respect of persons; there would be a spate of delations and denunciations. It was to be expected then that a high proportion of the stay-behind agents would hand themselves over and form a body of new double-cross agents operating in the theatre of war.

All these reasons carried weight, but the most potent reason for abolishing the double-cross system was a more general one. It was in fact that a wave of rather uninformed optimism carried away the judgment of many people; there was a widespread belief that the war must be over before the end of the year, and that it was high time to disembarrass ourselves of all these war commitments and complications.

The arguments against abolishing the system were, however, more powerful than those in favour of doing so. In the first place the fact that the deception "held" for so long after the invasion made it necessary to carry on the work at least until all possible advantage had been sucked from that particular plan. But furthermore, the end of OVERLORD deception did not in the least imply the end of all deception. It should in candour be admitted that the success of June 1944 had gone a little to our heads, and that we were therefore inclined to despise less spectacular but still not unimportant undertakings. Deceiving the enemy did not consist solely in putting over a carefully prepared detailed scheme; a simple directive to exaggerate or to minimise the forces available in this country would alone be sufficient to open up a line of useful work for us. And more than this. Was it really certain that we had seen the end of the period of strategic deception? The fortress of Europe had been successfully stormed, but might not the storming of the

fortress of Germany require another operation, equally difficult and equally needing a cover plan to support it?

Other arguments reinforced the same view. On closer
inspection the argument that we should concentrate on the
stay-behind agents appeared very thin. In fact, operations,
especially air operations, were still based to a large extent
on this country; in fact also the further back in the theatre
of war you go for your information, the more reliable and
valuable it is likely to be. The Germans were unlikely to
give the same confidence to newly established and untried
agents as they gave to the veterans of the old organisation.
Also the new agents in Europe could at best be expected
to be used mainly for short-time tactical work and could
hardly be built up for long-time service.

Nor was it certain that the use of the agents would
necessarily disappear with the conclusion of hostilities in
Europe. We could not tell in 1944 exactly how the end of
the war would come, and it seemed at least possible that
the Germans might continue to keep some sort of underground organisation alive for espionage even after miltary
defeat. After the 1914-1918 war the peace treaty had
stipulated that they might not maintain an information service, though they were allowed to keep a counterespionage
service; in fact they did maintain some sort of espionage service under various guises, chiefly of a commercial nature. The
same thing might occur once more, and in that case our
agents could be invaluable in disclosing the enemy's actions.
Indeed as the deception advantages of the double-cross
system receded, the counterespionage and intelligence advantages revived. Evidence of enemy intentions, code and
cypher knowledge, and even political propaganda began to
come to the front. They will be mentioned later in this
narrative.

The main and overwhelming argument for the retention
of the agents still remains to be stated. It was that we had
in the double-cross system a weapon of war which had
proved itself useful, and that the war was not yet over. Most
people were fond of asserting that they would never repeat
the follies of 1918, when safeguards had been prematurely

removed; but many seemed ready enough to make precisely the old mistake with regard to double-cross agents. In fact it was utterly impossible in 1944, just as at any other time, to fortell the future; and no one could tell if, or exactly how, the agents would be of use in the concluding period of the war. Yet all previous experience went to show that they would be useful, probably in a manner and for a purpose not accurately forecast by us. As the event proved, this expectation was entirely fulfilled.

Fortunately the arguments for maintaining our system prevailed; it was agreed to carry on and to adapt the system as required to the changing needs of the situation. It was also agreed that the new agents procured in Europe from the stay-behind organisation should be worked by officers in the field and controlled by Twenty-first and Twelfth Army Groups. Since the bulk of their work would probably be short-time and tactical in nature, and since it would be a practical impossibility to pass their traffic through the machine in this country, it came about that a new committee, the 212 Committee, was formed in August 1944 by Twenty-first and Twelfth Army Groups on the model of the Twenty Committee. The objects of the Committee, which was afterwards taken over by SHAEF, were to approve traffic for controlled agents, to direct the deception policy governing the traffic, and to authorise the use of controlled agents for particular operations. The Committee ran all double-cross agents on the Continent and continued to operate successfully until the conclusion of hostilities. Meantime the old system continued in this country.

It was remarked above that it was fortunate that the double-cross system was not prematurely dissolved; the fortune lay in the fact that two highly important and quite unexpected pieces of deception had to be undertaken in this last period. Both were successful and either alone would have amply justified the maintenance of a much larger system than was ours. One was connected with V-bombs and rockets and the other with the German U-boat campaign, and both will be described at the end of this chapter. Curiously, perhaps, the deception connected with general military plans was small, and most of it was carried out by agents in Europe, though GARBO did a considerable amount to clean up the notional formations, to convince the Germans that, when the offensive of Twenty-first Army Group was imminent, the contemplated airborne operation would take place between Cologne and Dusseldorf, and, after the crossing of the Rhine, to retain German reinforcements in the northwest under threat of an operation there. We shall return to deception work later, after the general history of the agents between the summer of 1944 and the end of hostilities has been considered.

As was only natural, the number of agents sank very considerably during this period. At the beginning of 1944 we had some twenty channels to the Germans of which nine were w/t; a year later there were only six active of which four were w/t. Lack of suitability for deception, failure to secure payment, a loss of interest on the part of the Germans, compromised reputation (as in the case of MUTT and JEFF, who had at long last come to the end of their many "invasions" of Norway) and, in the later stages, capture of German spy-masters were among the reasons which caused this decline in numbers.

What is remarkable is that no single case was compromised by the grand deception for OVERLORD, but that, on the contrary, those agents who took a leading part in it were more highly regarded by the Germans after it than before. Some of the cases, both those which survived and those which disappeared, deserve some mention. To SNIPER the Germans wished to send a transmitting set, and they made several tentative efforts to accomplish this purpose. He was in fact a Belgian airman, and when the Germans were informed that he was likely to be posted back to his own country, they changed their plan and proposed to leave a set for him in his own country. The set was successfully located, SNIPER returned to Belgium, and in January 1945 he reported to the Germans that he had gained possession of the set. He thus passed out of our hands to Twenty-first Army Group and became a useful wireless double agent under their control.

TREASURE turned out not to belie her name. She had arrived with only secret ink as a method of communication; but in March of 1944 she was sent to Lisbon in the hope that she might be given a wireless transmitter. The hope was fulfilled, and on her return wireless communication was established. Later it became necessary to operate the transmitter in her name using our own operator, partly because she was in poor health and partly because she proved exceptionally temperamental and troublesome.

When Paris was liberated we allowed TREASURE, whose set was being worked by an operator, to return to France in the French ATS. In August the German Abwehr officer who ran the case was captured and was brought to England as a prisoner of war. TREASURE was therefore in France and her spy-master in England; but wireless communications continued as though TREASURE was still here and her spy-master in Europe! The traffic of TREASURE as well as that of BRUTUS was of the greatest assistance to those watching the activities of the French network.*

A new case was that of SHEPHERD, a Frenchman, who arrived in March 1944. In itself the case was not important, for SHEPHERD could only report by secret writing and had no means of receiving messages from the Germans. But the method of recruitment and our reasons for accepting the case were peculiar. There was in Spain a German talent spotter and recruiter for Ast Hamburg named NETTLE, who was also in fact an agent working on behalf of M.I.6. NETTLE proposed to introduce into the German service, especially for work in America, agents who would in fact be friendly to the Allies. He had not been altogether successful

---

*A message from the department concerned dated 26 May 1944 shows the importance of the traffic of the agents in this respect: "I should like you . . . to know how much we appreciate the assistance you are giving us in respect of TREASURE and BRUTUS traffic. I have discussed the matter again this morning with the people actually on the job, and I find that about 30 percent of our success with the whole French network has been due solely to TREASURE and BRUTUS; experience in using the material will certainly raise this proportion even higher. It is seldom that we get such a stroke of luck in this job, especially with traffic so valuable as our French network: so I thought it right that you should know what a high degree of importance we at this end attribute to BRUTUS and TREASURE."

in his efforts, and it was therefore thought that the recruitment and operation of SHEPHERD would increase his prestige and restore German confidence in him. For this purpose alone, therefore, we took on the case and arranged for SHEPHERD to write a small number of letters.

Much more important among new cases was that of ROVER. He was a Pole who had earned his living as a subordinate railway official, a professional boxer, and a baker. After joining the Polish navy in the spring of 1939 and serving on land in the war he had been taken prisoner. Since then he had worked as a forced labourer and had been invited in June 1942 to join the German Secret Service. He had accepted in order to escape and had since then suffered many vicissitudes of fortune including visits to prison in almost every country in Europe. He eventually reached England via Spain in May 1944. His equipment consisted of microphotographs containing detailed instructions for constructing, and thereafter operating, a wireless transmitter, together with a complicated code, cover address, and secret ink. His instructions were to obtain employment in an aircraft factory and report upon the technical details of new aircraft.

What made him attractive to us was the fact that he had had a year's training in morse, the construction of wireless sets, and secret writing; we could not believe that the Germans would lavish so much care on someone in whom they did not believe. Consequently we housed him with one of our wireless operators, allowed him to begin the construction of a set, and meantime let him write to the Germans according to his instructions. To our surprise and disappointment the Germans did not respond after the letters had been written; in September, therefore, we decided to discontinue the case and to send ROVER back to the Polish navy, to which he technically belonged.

We were no doubt too impatient, for hardly had this been done when the Germans started to call ROVER. It was decided that a risk must be taken, and our own operator was put on to transmit as ROVER since he was conversant with all the latter's wireless habits. The impersonation was entirely successful, and two-way communication was established on 9 October. Unfortunately the operator was compelled to go to hospital in November and a plan had to be worked out to explain the consequent silence of ROVER's set. Worse was to follow, for the operator died, leaving us with the alternative of closing down the case or attempting a second impersonation. In the meantime the case had become important because of the necessities of our V-bomb and rocket deception, and consequently the second alternative was adopted. A second operator undertook to copy the style of the first operator, who had in his turn been copying ROVER, and contact was reestablished in January. In the first message from the new operator ROVER stated that he had been knocked down by a lorry in the blackout on 14 November and removed to hospital, where he had been found to be suffering from broken ribs, a dislocated collarbone, and internal injuries. Our medical adviser assured us that these injuries would suitably explain the length of ROVER's sojourn in hospital and we felt confident that any alteration in style in transmitting would be attributed by the Germans to the damage done to his shoulder. So far as we could tell no suspicion was aroused and the case continued satisfactorily till the conclusion of hostilities.

Another addition to the team in 1944 was an old friend. News had trickled through to us of a mysterious figure at Oslo—a man speaking bad German in a rather loud high-pitched voice, clad in a pepper-and-salt suit, displaying two gold teeth and enjoying the amenities of a private yacht. This we thought must be ZIGZAG, and so it was. He was dropped for the second time by parachute in Cambridgeshire at the end of June, together with two wireless sets, cameras, £6,000, and instructions for an espionage mission. Since he had left us he had been royally treated by his German masters, and most of his time had been spent as a kind of honorary consultant in sabotage methods in the Stelle at Oslo.* He had been lavishly paid and had, in his

---

*The Germans usually handled their agents with real psychological skill and insight. Thus ZIGZAG's vanity had been cleverly fed by his being accepted as a member of the officers' mess at the Nantes Stelle, and by Graumann's personal care for and attraction to him.

own opinion at least entirely hoodwinked the enemy; he
had among other tests completely satisfied a psychologist
with a pronounced American accent who had questioned
him at length before his second journey.

The chief objects of his mission were:

1. to procure photographs or plans of our Asdic gear for
   spotting submarines;
2. to ascertain details of the radio location system employed
   for the detection of planes, particularly as fitted to night
   fighters;
3. to report on damage caused by flying bombs;
4. to ascertain the location of American air force stations,
   since the Germans believed that certain American aerodromes dealt with the bombing of specific towns in
   Germany;
5. to get information about a new wireless frequency, since
   the Germans believed that we had a new frequency in
   which a new type of valve played an important part and
   that this might upset their V-2 weapon.

On completion of his tasks ZIGZAG was to return to Germany. He brought with him also a good deal of information,
notably about the new German weapons. The Germans were
relying on the flying bombs; but should these fail them they
would use "radio-operated rockets, bigger than the P-plane,
very costly in fuel and not economical in construction." He
told us that Berlin "resembled the ruins of Pompeii"; that
Goebbels's propaganda had persuaded the Germans that
London was a shambles, but that this propaganda was now
stretched to the utmost; that the morale of I. Marine was
particularly low owing to the British anti-U-boat devices;
and that petrol, he thought, was specially short in Germany.
In the event of success in his mission ZIGZAG was promised
about RM.800,000.

It would be pleasant to be able to record that ZIGZAG's
second innings was as profitable as his first, but such was
not the case. He was useful in transmitting information
about bomb damage and seems to have held his place in
German confidence; but he developed a dangerous tendency

to talk about his work and his achievements, and it therefore became necessary to terminate the case.

The BRUTUS case came to an end for different reasons.
Arrests and trials in France threatened enquiry into the
breakup of BRUTUS's early organisation in France and into
the conduct of the persons concerned, and it was considered
impossible to maintain the case longer. The GARBO network,
however, maintained itself to the end—indeed its ramifi-
cations increased in the last year of the war. A Wren, Agent
No. 7/3, was sent to Ceylon, where she worked on the staff
at Lord Louis Mountbatten's headquarters. Thence she
sent secret letters to GARBO which were forwarded to the
Germans by the courier. There is evidence to show that the
information contained in these letters was passed by the
Germans to the Japanese military attaché in Berlin, and
that he in turn sent it on to Tokyo.

Agent No. 4, who up to the time of OVERLORD had been
one of GARBO's main sources of information and who had
been compelled through his excess of zeal in the search for
news to desert from the N.A.A.F.I., ultimately "escaped"
to Canada. Here he made contact with Agent No. 5 and
set himself up as a wireless operator for Agent No. 5's network. With wireless facilities, the Canadian organisation
greatly appreciated in German eyes. They provided a highly
complicated security plan for transmissions and a very high
grade cypher. Wireless communications of the organisation
worked not only to London, but also directly between Canada and Madrid. Thus a weapon was prepared which could
be used if required for deception against the Japanese or for
counterespionage purposes against Germany in the New
World, if a postwar Germany attempted to continue or
inaugurate espionage activities there.

GARBO's personal credit remained high with both his real
and his pseudo friends. On the British side he was awarded
the M.B.E. in December 1944; on the German side, an
award of the Iron Cross was agreed to in June, in spite of
the fact that he was a Spanish national. A hitch, however,
subsequently occurred in making the actual award, and the
following message from Madrid to Berlin of 29 December

1944, which has subsequently come into our hands, well illustrates not only the reputation enjoyed by GARBO, but also the trials and difficulties which all case officers—British or German—had to undergo. It also provides some proof, if proof were needed, of the complete acceptance by the Germans of the picture of GARBO and his organisation which was prepared for them:

29.12.44.

In re award of Iron Cross II to GARBO and the discussions in Berlin. In our message of the 17.6. we applied for award of Iron Cross II to GARBO emphasising that he was a Spanish national, but giving as justification the fact that activity of GARBO in England constantly at the price of his life was just as important as the service at the front of the Spanish members of the Blue Division. We were informed in your message of the 24.6 that award was agreed to and that the submission of the prescribed proposal had been put forward. On the basis of this information we at this end were under the impression that no difficulties were to be expected in [obtaining] the eventual award, and this was reported to GARBO, who was at that time, as a result of very great difficulties, in a state of mental depression for psychological reasons. The communication of this news about the award had the expected result and evoked from GARBO a written expression of his special pride at the distinction. Difficulties in maintaining and extending the GARBO network have been constantly increasing recently, but were mastered by GARBO with an utter disregard for all personal interests and by giving all he was capable of. GARBO has himself been in hiding for weeks, separated from wife and children. The extraordinary successes of GARBO have been made possible by his constant, complete, and express confidence in the Fuehrer and our cause. He regards the award of the Iron Cross II, as reported to him, as final and as coming from the Fuehrer. It seems psychologically impossible now to inform him that the award will not be made without exercising the most adverse effect on him and his organisation. For the reasons stated please support the award from your end with all possible means. Would it not be possible to classify GARBO retrospectively as a member of the Blue Division? Please report to us by w/t results of your efforts, as GARBO has already asked for the decoration in question to be sent to his next of kin to be kept for him.

One more new activity in 1945 should be mentioned in this place—the development of double-cross agents in Gibraltar. The conditions of work there made it necessary that a large number of workmen should enter the fortress and dockyard each day, and this gave a magnificent opportunity to the enemy for espionage. To provide complete security against this danger was impossible, but it was found practicable to penetrate the enemy organisation by the use of double agents. For these traffic became more and more difficult, and in consequence the Twenty Committee was asked, and agreed, to approve sufficient information in London to maintain the agents on a good level.

Throughout the period of the invasion of Europe and the military victories the stream of traffic of our agents continued to give a picture of German interests and German intentions. Probably no good purpose would be served here by an analysis of the questions which were asked such as that attempted in chapter 5, but it may be worthwhile to indicate in general terms the sort of questions which were being asked during the last six months of 1944. First and foremost it must be remembered that the Germans were entirely on the defensive, and therefore their prime need was information about the force and direction of the blows which were to be launched against them. Thus details of armies and order of battle comprise a very high proportion of the questions, together with requests for information about the direction of the offensives; in September, for example, uneasiness about Norway came again to the fore. Personal questions were asked about high-ranking officers, particularly those connected with the air force and airborne troops, and political questions indicated a keen desire to learn of any possible differences of opinion between Russia and the other Allies. In matters of production chief weight was laid on aircraft production and chemical factories, but a cessation of questions about gas warfare indicated clearly both that the Germans had abandoned any intention they might have had of adopting this method of warfare and were satisfied that we should not adopt it either.

Airborne forces were a constantly recurring subject, and one question in December—"American Airborne Divisions 82 and 101, probably in the district Châlons-sur-Marne, to what extent are they ready for combat?"—seems to point to Rundstedt's Ardennes offensive which occurred very shortly afterwards. With regard to aircraft there were a number of questions on jet propulsion, and specific questions were asked about the Halifax, Corsair, Sunderland, Super Fortress, Seafire, and Midnight Mauler. There was naturally a lessening of interest in our antiaircraft defences, apart from messages relating to V-1 and V-2. Antisubmarine devices excited considerable interest, as did German fear of "reprisals" on the British side in the shape of "flying bombs" and "rocket planes." Ports and concentrations of shipping had their place, chiefly in connection with new or projected invasion. A great number of questions concerned the fall and results of flying bombs and rockets, but these will be mentioned later; they were sent to all the agents who were actively at work.

A most interesting question of detail having regard to later developments was sent to GELATINE on 2 November: "In which part of London is the Uranium Research Institute, in charge of Professor Lise Meitner, a Jewish emigrant, in conjunction with Professor O. R. Frisch?" It is relevant to note in this connection that already in April 1942 TRICYCLE, then in America, had had an enquiry with regard to research on the atomic bomb. His question of that date, obviously badly translated for him from the German, ran as follows:

Decay of Uran. According to some information obtained, there is reason to believe that the scientific works for the utilization of the atomic-kernel energy are being driven forward into a certain direction in the U.S. partly by use of helium. Continuous informations about the tests made on this subject are required and particularly: (1) What process is practised in the U.S. for the sending of heavy uran? (2) Where are being made tests with more important quantities of uran? (Universities, industrial laboratories, etc.) (3) Which other raw materials are being used at these tests? It is to be recommended to entrust only best experts with this test, and if not available, to abstain from it.

Before leaving this topic we should restate a conviction which established itself more and more firmly in our minds —viz., that a careful and intelligent study of all the traffic could and would have given an accurate picture of all the more important German interests and intentions throughout the war. In retrospect it is clear that more use could have been made of this product of double-cross agents' work.

Finally we come to the last two pieces of important deception carried out by the help of our agents, those deceptions in fact mentioned earlier in this chapter. The first was connected with V-bombs and rockets, and was an issue which in the earlier days we had not considered in connection with deception. It turned out, however, since our team was ready to tackle any such job, to be a task for which the agents were particularly well fitted, and one which lent itself readily to deception uses.

Quite early we had become alive to the possible use of so-called secret weapons by the Germans, and we learned in fact a great deal about their probable nature and the extent of the menace through the traffic of the agents. In July 1943 Home Forces reported to the Twenty Committee that they were laying on certain security measures to deal with the possible use of rockets by the Germans, and asked to be informed of any developments which might come to our notice; in August D.N.I. considered the question of long-range rockets of such importance that he proposed that the Twenty Committee should go into the whole question in detail with a view to using the agents to gain further information about this matter. In particular he thought that it might be possible to discuss what part of the German plans was deception and what part was real. It was, however, agreed that this was really a matter for M.I.6 and for the Sandys Committee, and C.S.S. told D.N.I. that assistance at this stage was not needed.

In September ARTIST warned TRICYCLE not to live in London because of the rockets which were to be fired at it from positions on the French coast, and this information was transmitted to C. for retransmission to the Sandys Committee. At the end of the month it was decided that TRICYCLE should not be sent to Lisbon since M.I.6 could by then communicate directly with ARTIST, and it was subsequently agreed that we should use ARTIST to the full for this purpose and not attempt to use HAMLET, who had also been suggested as a possible source of information. GARBO was also turned on to ask cautious questions, since it was felt that, if the Germans really had a devastating weapon for use against London, they would not risk the loss of the GARBO network by allowing GARBO to continue to live in a highly dangerous area. The answers received were on the whole reassuring, and allowed us to assume that the threat was not imminent and that, if the attack came, it would not be greatly more severe than previous bombing attacks of the old variety.*

At the beginning of 1944, when German air raids were intensified and when many questions were asked of the agents about their effects, a policy for reply was agreed upon. Reports were to be substantially accurate, but damage was to be minimised; the effect on morale was to be represented as finding expression in a demand for more raids on Germany; the location of damage was to be substantially accurate, but not so detailed as to disclose the

---

*The answer did, however, warn GARBO that the attack would take place, and the Germans actually reminded him in June 1944 of their warning in the previous December.

pattern of damage in a particular area; as little reference as possible was to be made to unexploded bombs; and attempts were to be made to discover if these raids were or were not the special danger of which some agents had been warned. In March it was considered by H.D.E. that incendiary bombs were less damaging than H.E., and the agents were consequently for the time being to attempt to give the contrary impression.

Early in June the first flying bombs (V-1) arrived and the agents were soon asked to report upon them in detail. Here at once an opportunity for deception presented itself. However the flying bombs were worked, it was clear that the Germans could only correct their aim and secure results by adjustments based on experiment, and that their data must rest in the main upon reports from this country. The agents could not fail to report on incidents which occurred under their noses, and which were common knowledge in England. If, for example, St. Paul's was hit, it was useless and harmful to report that the bomb had descended upon a cinema in Islington, since news of the truth would inevitably get through to Germany in a short space of time.* In other words, it was necessary to decide what measure of useful deception was possible without blowing the agents.

It was soon realised that widely scattered though they were, the majority of the bombs were falling two or three miles short of Trafalgar Square, and the general plan of deception soon took shape. It was, in brief, to attempt to induce the Germans still further to shorten their range by exaggerating the number of those bombs which fell to the north and west of London and keeping silent, when possible, about those in the south and east. The general effect would be that the Germans would suppose that they tended to overshoot and would therefore shorten their range, whereas in fact they already tended to undershoot. The danger was

---

*At a later stage great danger was caused to our deception by the publication in the evening papers of maps showing the fall of bombs in various London boroughs.

that we could not be sure that the Germans had not a method of themselves accurately locating the fall of bombs, and this compelled caution on our side.

The Chiefs of Staff approved the proposed deception policy but some civilian departments raised objections and a considerable controversy arose which hampered our plans. Briefly, the Chiefs of Staff took the hard-headed view that, since the bombs must fall somewhere if not shot down *en route*, it was best to divert them as much as possible from the most thickly populated area; unfortunately the Cabinet took the view that "it would be a serious matter to assume any direct degree of responsibility for action which would affect the areas against which flying bombs were aimed," and consequently rejected the plan. The Chiefs of Staff, however, resubmitted the proposal and eventually in mid-August we secured, though in somewhat grudging terms, the directive which we required. We were to "continue to convey to the enemy information which will confirm his belief that he has no need to lengthen his range . . . and within limits to take such steps as [we might] judge to intensify this belief."

Another factor arrested our operations. We received a steady stream of information passed to the enemy by uncontrolled sources, mainly OSTRO. Although the information was almost entirely false, it was believed by the Germans, and we therefore plotted all this material graphically in order to arrive at a mean point of impact (M.P.I.). We then passed across such information as was necessary to correct the inferences from OSTRO's material and bring the overall M.P.I. to the desired point.

Early in September the rocket attacks (V-2) started, and presented us with similar problems and similar opportunities to those connected with V-1. Consequently our deception was also on similar lines. There was, however, a technical difference. In the flying bomb attacks location had been the important factor because it was doubtful whether the enemy could tie the times we gave them to particular shots; in the rocket attacks timings were vital because the enemy could calculate accurately the time of arrival of any shot, and link this up with any information which we gave him. It was therefore decided to give real incidents which would show an M.P.I. in Central London, but to give as the times for these incidents the times of shots falling some five to eight miles short. In this way over a period of some months we contrived to encourage the enemy steadily to diminish his range; thus in the four weeks from 20 January to 17 February 1945 the real M.P.I. moved eastward about two miles a week and ended well outside the boundary of London region.*

The deception practised with regard to flying bombs and rockets was entirely the work of H.D.E.; we had nothing to do with its policy or details, but, as in the case of strategic deception, we provided the channels through which the desired misinformation could be sent to the enemy. The deception was ample justification for keeping the agents alive after the invasion of France, more particularly as the less important agents were the most useful for this purpose. ROVER, for example, could be used freely because he had no connection with the rest and because his collapse, if blatant untruth had to be risked, would not necessarily affect the others. Letter-writing agents were also used to confirm the accounts given by the w/t agents.

It would be only fair to claim that the deception was a very real triumph for H.D.E. In spite of a good deal of opposition they succeeded in pushing through their policy, and succeeded also, if we may judge by results, in causing the Germans to shorten their range considerably. When a report was made to the W. Board on the year's work of double-cross agents after the conclusion of hostilities, D.M.I. gave a brief summary of a document which he had recently received. This was an appreciation by a scientific expert who had calculated the approximate extra number of lives which would have been lost had the Germans'

*A captured German map shows a schedule of results for a fortnight based on agents' reports and gives the M.P.I. in the Charing Cross area. This was, of course, exactly what we wished the enemy to believe.

M.P.I. been five miles further west each week than it was. The expert had no knowledge of our work and supposed that the location of the M.P.I. was simply due to German miscalculation. We, however, were surely entitled to feel that the double-cross system had done its full share in the saving of those many thousands of lives.

The last important work carried out by double-cross agents was on behalf of the Admiralty. It should here be remarked that since the earliest days the Admiralty had made use of a double-cross system for purposes of deception and that, in the nature of the case, they had been able to do so without reference to other departments. A military deception of use for a continued operation needed a great deal of coordination, but a deception with regard to submarine warfare or convoys could be, and was, carried through by the Admiralty alone. For convenience such work was often referred to as *ad hoc* deception, and in some instances it was carried out very successfully and often over a long period. Thus, for example, a shipbuilding programme was put through so that the fleet could be enlarged, and this enabled the Admiralty to give two notional aircraft carriers to C.-in-C. East Indies in 1943 when in fact he had none.

There were also a number of deceptions in connection with North Russian convoys and fleet movements to carry out operations off Norway, and a number of others connected with weapons and methods used in antisubmarine warfare. An example of these was one connected with the use of antitorpedo nets by merchant vessels, which lasted from June 1941 to the end of the war. The details are unimportant; in broad outline the deception was based upon giving misinformation about the nets; upon disguising the basic principle that the torpedo was caught by the tail and not stopped by the head; and by considerably minimising the efficiency of the nets. What is important is that for some four years N.I.D. was able, through our agents, to pass muddling and untrue information on this topic to the Germans, to withhold from them up to the end of the war the actual principle of our antitorpedo nets,* thus preventing them from adopting the fairly simple countermeasures which they might have used, and to gain by direct evidence and inference some indication of what they were themselves doing in this special department.

The culmination of specifically naval deceptions through double-cross agents came in 1945, and was implemented through TATE. Towards the end of the previous year the U-boat war became rapidly more menacing. For some time radar and intensive air patrols had made it almost impossible for U-boats to operate close inshore round the British Isles where otherwise they would have hunted to the best advantage. But now a new factor altered the situation: the U-boat no longer had to came to the surface to recharge batteries, etc., as the Schnorkel enabled it to do this under water. This assisted the U-boat because it could lie in wait for a long period in a suitable area, and the only really effective counterstroke was the laying of deep minefields which would catch the U-boat but over which the surface craft could safely pass. Unfortunately shortage both of mines and mine-layers in home waters made it difficult to exploit this countermeasure fully.

In the circumstances D.N.I. was asked to attempt to convince the Germans that there were far more minefields than in fact there were, and for this purpose TATE was brought into play. At an earlier stage in his career he had procured information from a "friend" who was known as his "mine-laying friend." This acquaintanceship was now revived and the friend was freely entertained in TATE's London flat. He was notionally serving in H.M.S. *Plover*, which, together with H.M.S. *Apollo*, was in fact doing most of the real mine-laying, and he was thus able, when not at sea, to allow a stream of information with regard to the new minefields to reach the Germans by way of TATE and his transmitter. The credibility of the information was confirmed by allowing TATE to give advance information of

*In spite of the fact that our merchant ships fitted with these nets visited neutral ports where German agents were numerous and active.

real U-boats which had been sunk by causes other than mining when it was known that the Germans were unaware of the details of the actual sinking. When such losses were corroborated by reports from the Red Cross of prisoner of war survivors and by other means, the stock of TATE's informant naturally rose in the estimation of the Germans.

It is unnecessary to enter into the details of this deception. What was done, in broad outline, was this. TATE reported piece by piece to the Germans the existence of a large number of new minefields which did not in fact exist. After various warnings given by the Germans to their U-boat commanders, a stroke of good fortune for us clinched the matter in the Germans' mind. A U-boat reported that it had been so damaged by a mine that it had had to scuttle itself, and this mine was in the general area of TATE's notional minefields. As the U-boat did not specify its position *precisely*, the Germans not unnaturally assumed the truth of all TATE's stories, and in consequence closed 3,600 square miles of the western approaches to U-boats. The exact credit balance of the deception cannot be assessed; but on a modest estimate TATE must have ensured the safety of many of our vessels which would otherwise have run considerable risks in that area, and it is not impossible that his misinformation moved U-boats from areas where they were safe to areas where they emphatically were not.

It is curious that the last two major deceptions carried out by double-cross agents—i.e., that connected with rockets and that connected with minefields—were deceptions the possibility of which could not by any means have been foreseen. They could be carried out, and were, simply because the agents had been kept in being, almost on the Micawber principle. Yet either of these deceptions alone by its beneficial results would have amply justified the system and the labour expended on it throughout the whole of the war.

The agents died hard. Among those communicating directly with Germany, TATE received a message from Hamburg sent at 17.50 hours on 2 May—a matter of hours before the fall of that city. The Germans ran true to form to the last, and taught us a lesson with this last message. In it they encouraged TATE, who had just sent them information about mine-laying in the Kola inlet, to maintain contact, presumably both with the mine-laying friend and with them. But further they replied to another question sent by TATE with regard to a suitcase containing private papers and valuables which he had left at Hamburg in 1939. This they said they had safely delivered to his sister in September 1944 after destroying all dangerous documents. If you wish agents to serve you well you must satisfy their personal wishes and personal interests; in their last message to TATE the Germans gave a shining example of how the good case officer should behave, and gave it too in circumstances which even the most phlegmatic must have admitted to have been a little trying!

13: CONCLUSION

If the preceding narrative has been reasonably clear there should be no need to summarise its contents. At any rate no attempt to do so will be made. A reader, however, who wishes to collect and resume his general impressions should at this point turn back to page 58 and reread what was there described as the creed of double cross; he should then reread also the last paragraph of chapter 1 (pp. 34 and 35). With these two short passages fresh in mind he has in fact the whole theory of double-cross.

A consideration of the theory and practice of double-cross though it may give legitimate cause for satisfaction, also gives rise to one somewhat disturbing thought—indeed this thought must have obtruded itself into the mind of any judicious reader very early in his perusal of this book. The disturbing, perhaps even alarming, thought is this. We are sure that we deceived the Germans and turned their weapon against themselves; can we be quite sure that they were not equally successful in turning our weapon against us? Now our double-cross agents were the straight agents of the Germans—their whole espionage system in the U.K. What did the Germans gain from this system? The answer cannot be doubtful. They gained no good whatever from their agents, and they did take from them a very great deal of harm. It would be agreeable to be able to accept the simple explanation, to sit back in the armchair of complacency, to say that we were very clever and the Germans very stupid, and that consequently we gained both on the swings and the roundabouts as well. But that argument just won't hold water at all.

What evidence there is goes to show that the Germans were at least our equals in all the arts connected with espionage and counterespionage. They had studied the subject over a long period; after some early clumsy improvisations they settled down to train their agents carefully; they certainly handled many of them with admirable psychological understanding; they supported them loyally and rewarded them adequately; in short there is no reason whatever to attribute our success and German failure to our superior wisdom or our greater ability or our better practical handling of the agents. In one respect, however, and in one which is not immediately obvious, we can and should claim a great advantage.

This, curiously enough, (curiously, because we were not dealing with straightforward matters), was the personal integrity of all officers and other persons concerned in the U.K. from the top to the bottom. Almost always when a real blunder was made by the Germans it was traceable to the fact that the Abwehr official implicated was governed by *personal* considerations; he was making money out of the agent or gaining prestige from him or even only making his post in some comfortable neutral haven secure, and in consequence he could not and would not judge the agent and the agent's work, dispassionately or even honestly. Many an organisation during the war has been described as "a racket," sometimes rightly and sometimes wrongly. What is clear is that no racket is going to prosper over a long period, and that in all secret intelligence work absolute personal integrity of all concerned and the exclusion of all personal considerations is the first and fundamental condition of success.

We are a little but only little nearer to resolving the difficulty suggested in the last paragraph. A more substantial reason to explain why the double-cross system succeeded and the German espionage system in the U.K. failed might be found in the simple proposition that in time of war espionage in an enemy country is doomed to failure because the dice are hopelessly loaded against the spy. This surely is difficult to deny—unpalatable though the admission may be. It is not of course denied that in countries *occupied* by the enemy the straight agent may perform great services; assisted by resistance movements or even only by the passive goodwill of a large part of the population he may be able to carry out acts of sabotage, to collect and transmit information, or even to assist revolutionary movements. But in enemy country his case must be almost hopeless. Suspicion is rife, and is aroused at once by the least interest shown in military or semimilitary undertakings; security checks abound and identity documents must be proof against examination; the transmission of any information presents almost insuperable difficulties.

We do not know what was in fact gained by straight agents in Germany during the war, and it is always dangerous to generalise without the facts. But we do know that German straight agents in England gained less than nothing for their masters, and it is safe to say that in theory at any rate we could hope for only very meagre advantages from our agents in Germany. In fact the general conclusion is inescapable. Espionage in wartime is difficult and usually unprofitable; counterespionage is comparatively easy and may yield satisfactory results. In peacetime the boot is on the other foot. A spy who is prepared to take his time and observe all reasonable precautions is extraordinarily hard to catch and may obtain information of the highest value. On the other hand counterespionage in peacetime is a matter of the utmost difficulty; it is immensely hard to secure proof: it is impossible to act on suspicion however strong; the whole tenour of life in this country is antagonistic to overregimentation and to rigid classification; it is better to let many spies "run" rather than to risk one mistake. So we come to this provisional—and admittedly theoretical—conclusion: in peacetime espionage is easy and profitable, counterespionage is difficult and unrewarding; in wartime espionage is difficult and usually unprofitable; counterespionage is comparatively easy and yields the richest returns.

There is a practical conclusion as well, which concerns the relations of M.I.6 and the Security Service. Espionage and counterespionage deal with different sides of the same problems and often with the same persons. How is it possible to avoid the conclusion that the two services must, if they are to be fully effective, be united as closely as organisational arrangements permit? At the very least they should base their activities on records completely accessible to each. That is an argument which could be developed at length—but not here. It leads on to the problems of the whole organisation of intelligence in the future.

APPENDIX 1:
DOUBLE-CROSS AGENTS
IN THE UNITED KINGDOM

There are personal files dealing with about 120 double-cross agents in M.I.5 records. Many of the cases never developed, others were of no great importance, and some, such as COBWEB and BEETLE in Iceland and MOONBEAM in Canada, did not operate from the U.K. It would therefore serve no useful purpose to make mention of all the cases. The list which follows gives brief details of some of the more interesting of these cases which were operated from this country. In this list w/t stands for wireless telegraphy; s/w for communication in secret ink or by microphotography; p/c for personal contact in neutral or enemy countries.

Agent	Method of Communication	Main Tasks	Date of Starting Work	Date of Finishing Work	Reason for Conclusion of Case	Remarks
1. BALLOON	s/w	General, especially arms and armament	May 41	Nov. 43	Germans considered that other TRICYCLE connections made it unnecessary to continue with BALLOON	BALLOON might have done more if personal contact could have been arranged for him.
2. BRONX	s/w	Industrial and political information	Oct. 42	—	Still working at conclusion of hostilities	
3. BRUTUS	w/t	To create Polish fifth column in England and to report on military matters	Oct. 42	Jan. 45	Fear of disclosures in trials of French acquaintances of BRUTUS	An unpaid agent working for ideological reasons.
4. CARELESS	s/w	R.A.F. information, especially delivery of American aircraft. Also production of A.A. defences.	July 41	Jan. 43	Refused to continue to work	His personal conduct and the consequent impossibility of controlling him except in prison spoiled a promising case.
5. CARROT	—	Reports to Vichy Government	June 42	Dec. 42	Lack of interest on part of enemy	Purpose was really to discover if Vichy was trying to penetrate organisations here.
6. CELERY	p/c	Air Force matters	Jan. 41	Aug. 41	Misfortune	—
7. DRAGONFLY	w/t	Observation of aerodromes and troop movements. Daily weather reports; military and general information	Mar. 41	Jan. 44	German failure to pay agent	His messages were responsible for capture of the spy JOB.

Agent	Method of Communication	Main Tasks	Date of Starting Work	Date of Finishing Work	Reason for Conclusion of Case	Remarks
8. FATHER	s/w and reception by w/t	To steal a plane and return to Germany. All Air Force information, including technical matters	June 41	June 43	Questions became embarrassing to answer, and agent was posted overseas	—
9. FIDO	s/w (no method of reception)	To steal a plane and return. To send information on aviation, concentrations of troops, and technical matters	July 43	Feb. 44	Suspicions and bad communications	—
10. FREAK	w/t	General information and wireless messages on behalf of TRICYCLE	Dec. 43	May 44	Breakdown of TRICYCLE network	—
11. GANDER	w/t transmission only	Road obstacles and defences in northwest England and morale	Oct. 40	Nov. 40	Imperfect means of communication	—
12. GARBO	s/w w/t and courier	General information, especially military	Apr. 42	—	End of hostilities	See account of GARBO and his network in text.
13. GELATINE	s/w	Political information	May 41	May 45	Conclusion of hostilities	Started as a recruit found by TRICYCLE.
14. GIRAFFE	s/w	Mainly Air Force matters	Sep. 40	—	Insufficient traffic	—
15. G.W.	p/c and Spanish diplomatic bag	Sabotage. General information	Oct. 39	Feb. 42	Arrest of his Spanish contact	—

16. JEFF	w/t	Sabotage. General information	Apr. 41	Feb. 44	Doubts about German belief in the case	See MUTT. JEFF was imprisoned from Aug. 41 onwards.
17. JOSEF	p/c and courier	Shipping and convoys	Aug. 42	Dec. 44	Failure to extract sufficient advantage from it	One of several seamen agents writing to the Japanese at Lisbon.
18. LIPSTICK	s/w	Troop disposition and technical information	Nov. 42	Mar. 44	Complications due to his Catalan activities	—
19. METEOR	s/w	General information, especially naval	Apr. 43	May 44	Breakdown of TRICYCLE network	Started with two types of letters, controlled and uncontrolled, owing to German attempt at triple cross.
20. MULLET	s/w and p/c	General information, especially production and industrial	Dec. 41	May 44	Doubts about communications	Worked to HAMLET in Lisbon.
21. MUTT	w/t	Sabotage and general, especially military information	Apr. 41	Feb. 44	Doubts about German belief in the case	See JEFF.
22. PEPPERMINT	s/w sent in diplomatic bag	General information, especially morale, military, factories, and aircraft production	Dec. 41	April 43	Breakdown of communications	Worked to Alcazar. Revival attempted in March 1944.
23. PUPPET	s/w	General, especially economic	Apr. 43	May 44	Doubts about communications	HAMLET's representative in England.
24. RAINBOW	s/w	Reports on aviation, air defence, industrial, and economic matters	Feb. 40	June 43	Weakening of German interest	Connected with prewar agents.

Agent	Method of Communication	Main Tasks	Date of Starting Work	Date of Finishing Work	Reason for Conclusion of Case	Remarks
25. ROVER	s/w and w/t	Details of aircraft factory. Air raid damage	May 44	May 45	Conclusion of hostilities	—
26. SHEPHERD	s/w (no method of reception)	Suppliers and manufacturers, attitude of miners and railway employees, and coastal information	Dec. 43	—	—	Run in order to support NETTLE in Spain.
27. SNARK, THE	s/w	Food prices and living conditions	July 41	Mar. 43	Lack of German interest	—
28. SNIPER	s/w and w/t	Aircraft and scientific apparatus, and methods used in antisubmarine warfare	Nov. 43	May 45	End of hostilities	Handed over to Twenty-first Army Group in Dec. 1944.
29. SNOW	w/t and p/c	General, especially Air Force matters	Sep. 39	Mar. 41	See text	—
30. SUMMER	w/t	General on area round Birmingham	Sep. 40	Jan. 41	Agent's attempt to escape	—
31. SWEET WILLIAM	Spanish diplomatic bag	Morale, food situation, etc.	Aug. 41	Aug. 42	Method of communication unsatisfactory owing to lack of control	—
32. TATE	w/t	General information (see text)	Sep. 40	May 45	End of hostilities	Operated for more than four and half years.
33. TEAPOT	w/t and p/c	General	Jan. 43	1945	No further use	A triple cross who provided useful information for the Admiralty.

34. TREASURE	s/w and w/t	Military information and news about projected invasion	Aug. 43	Dec. 44	No further use	See text.
35. TRICYCLE	p/c, s/w, and w/t	General, military, and economic information	Dec. 40	May 44	Arrest of ARTIST made all TRICYCLE group suspect	Worked in U.S.A. as well as in U.K. See text.
36. WASHOUT	s/w	Troop dispositions and aircraft production	June 42	Dec. 42	German lack of interest and unsatisfactory character of the agent	—
37. WEASEL	s/w	General and naval	May 42	Dec. 42	German failure to reply	We suspected that he contrived to warn the Germans.
38. WORM, THE	s/w	Military, naval, and Air Force information	July 43	Jan. 44	German lack of interest probably due to length of time spent in reaching England	—
39. ZIGZAG	w/t	Sabotage. Movements of U.S. troops. Anti-U-boat devices and night fighter radio location devices	Dec. 42	Nov. 44	Lack of security on part of the agent	Dropped twice by parachute in England in Dec. 1942 and June 1944.

APPENDIX 2:
TRICYCLE'S AMERICAN QUESTIONNAIRE

(Translation)

Naval Information.—Reports on enemy shipments (material food-stuffs—combination of convoys, if possible with names of ships and speeds).

Assembly of troops for oversea transport in U.S.A. and Canada. Strength—number of ships—ports of assembly—reports on ship building (naval and merchant ships)—wharves (dockyards)—state and private owned wharves— new works—list of ships being built or resp. having been ordered—times of building.

Reports regarding U.S.A. strong points of all descriptions especially in Florida—organisation of strong points for fast boats (E-boats) and their depot ships—coastal defence—organisation districts.

Hawaii.—Ammunition dumps and mine depots.

1. Details about naval ammunition and mine depot on the Isle of Kushua (Pearl Harbour). If possible sketch.

2. Naval ammunition depot Lualuelei. Exact position? Is there a railway line (junction)?

3. The total ammunition reserve of the army is supposed to be in the rock of the Crater Aliamanu. Position?

4. Is the Crater Punchbowl (Honolulu) being used as ammunition dump? If not, are there other military works?

Aerodromes.

1. *Aerodrome Lukefield.*— Details (sketch if possible) regarding the situation of the hangars (number?), workshops, bomb depots, and petrol depots. Are there underground petrol installations?—Exact position of the seaplane station? Occupation?

2. *Naval air arm strong point Kaneche.*—Exact report regarding position, number of hangars, depots, and workshops (sketch). Occupation?

3. *Army aerodromes Wicham Field and Wheeler Field.*—Exact position? Reports regarding number of hangars, depots and work-shops. Underground installations? (Sketch.)

4. *Rodger's Airport.*—In case of war, will this place be taken over by the army or the navy? What preparations have been made? Number of hangars? Are there landing possibilities for seaplanes?

5. *Airport of the Panamerican Airways.*—Exact position? (If possible sketch.) Is this airport possibly identical with Rodger's Airport or a part thereof? (A wireless station of the Panamerican Airways is on the Peninsula Mohapuu.)

Naval Strong Point Pearl Harbour.

1. Exact details and sketch about the situation of the state wharf, of the pier installations, workshops, petrol installations, situations of dry dock No. 1 and of the new dry dock which is being built.

2. Details about the submarine station (plan of situation). What land installations are in existence?

3. Where is the station for mine search formations [Minensuchverbaende]? How far has the dredger work progressed at the entrance and in the east and and southeast lock? Depths of water?

4. Number of anchorages [Liegeplaetze]?

5. Is there a floating dock in Pearl Harbour or is the transfer of such a dock to this place intended?

Special tasks.—Reports about torpedo protection nets newly introduced in the British and U.S.A. navy. How far are they already in existence in the merchant and naval fleet? Use during voyage? Average speed reduction when in use. Details of construction and others.

1. Urgently required are exact details about the armoured strengths of American armoured cars, especially of the types which have lately been delivered from the U.S.A. to the Middle East. Also all other reports on armoured cars and the composition of armoured (tank) formations are of greatest interest.

2. Required are the Tables of Organisation (TO) of the American infantry divisions and their individual units (infantry regiments, artillery "Abteilung," and so forth) as well as of the American armoured divisions and their individual units (armoured tank regiments, reconnaissance section, and so forth). These TO are lists showing strength, which are published by the American War Department and are of a confidential nature.

3. How is the new light armoured car (tank)? Which type is going to be finally introduced? Weight? Armament? Armour?

1. Position of British participations and credits in U.S.A. in June 1940. What are England's payment obligations from orders since the coming into force of the Lend Lease Bill? What payments has England made to U.S.A. since the outbreak of war for goods supplied, for establishment of works, for the production of war material, and for the building of new or for the enlargement of existing wharves?

2. Amount of state expenditure in the budget years 1939/40,

1940/41, 1941/42, 1942/43 altogether and in particular for the army and the rearmament.

3. Financing of the armament programme of the U.S.A. through taxes, loans and tax credit coupons. Participation of the Refico and the companies founded by it (Metal Reserve Corp., Rubber Reserve Corp., Defence Plant Corp., Defence Supplies Corp., Defence Housing Corp.) in the financing of the rearmament.

4. Increase of state debt and possibilities to cover this debt.

All reports on American air rearmament are of greatest importance. The answers to the following questions are of special urgency:

    I. How large is—
- (a) the total monthly production of aeroplanes?
- (b) the monthly production of bombers [Kampfflugzeuge]?
- (c)   "   "   "   " fighter planes?
- (d)   "   "   "   " training planes [Schulflugzeuge]?
- (e)   "   "   "   " civil aeroplanes [Zivilflugzeuge]?

    II. How many and which of these aeroplanes were supplied to the British Empire, that is to say—
- (a) to Great Britain?
- (b) to Canada?
- (c) to Africa?
- (d) to the Near East?
- (e) to the Far East and Australia?

    III. How many U.S.A. pilots finish their training monthly?

    IV. How many U.S.A. pilots are entering the R.A.F.?

Reports on Canadian Air Force are of great value.

All information about number and type (pattern) of front aeroplanes [Frontflugzeuge]. Quantity, numbers and position of the echellons [Staffeln] are of great interest. Of special importance is to get details about the current air training plan in Canada, that is to say: place and capacity of individual schools and if possible also their numbers. According to reports received every type of school (beginners'—advanced—and observer school) is numbered, beginning with 1.

INDEX

Abbreviations, list, xix

Abwehr, 38*n*, 151–52. *See also* German espionage system

Admiralty, 103, 135, 182

Africa, North, landings in, 109–11

Agents: case officers and, 21–23, 52; double life of, 68–69; establishing identity of, 14–15; in European countries, 75–76; Execution Committee, 66; financial arrangements, 25; German. *See* German espionage system; list and summary of, 190-95; preparation and building up, 9–10, 71–72; principles in dealing with, 17–33; psychological study of, 23–25; quality of, 32–33; questions asked of, 72–76, 124–25, 175–77; records of, 27–28; risks of, 28–30; traffic (messages passed through), 71–81; trustworthiness, 148; truthfulness and verisimilitude, 19–20

Aircraft and aerodromes: false information on, 83–84, 102–03; questions on, 74, 76–77, 124–25, 176

Alcazar de Velasco, Spanish agent, 57, 99, 113

Alexander, Lord, General, 134–35

Anderson, Sir John, 62

Antitorpedo nets, 182–83

Apollo, H.M.S., 183

ARTIST, 139–40, 153–54, 178

B.1.a., vii, xvii, 11, 14, 16, 17, 69, 101, 128, 149, 150*n*, 163, 164; organisation of, 62, 66; origin of,

61; plans, 82–89

BALLOON, 78, 79, 86, 96, 109, 138, 140

BASKET, 99–100

BEETLE, 114, 143

Berlin, agents in, 75, 76

Bevan, Colonel, 62*n*, 107–09, 137*n*

BISCUIT, 43–45, 50–51, 92

Blockade of Britain, 77–78

Boyle, Air Commodore, 61

Brest, agents in, 75, 76

Britische Kriegsheer, Das, 124

BRONX, 9, 120; in D Day preparations, 149, 161–62

Brussels, agents in, 75, 76

BRUTUS, 120–21, 140–42, 152, 169; background of, 140–42; in D Day preparations, 148–49, 155, 156; end of service, 173

B.U.F. (British Union of Fascists), 38

Busch, Major Friedrich, 86*n*

Calvo, Spanish attaché, 93, 113

Camp WX, 150

Canada, agents in, 173

Canaris, Admiral, 151

CARELESS, 97–98, 109, 143–44

Carl, Erich, 150

CARROT, 117

Case officers, 21–23, 52

Catalan Separatist movement, 131

Cavendish-Bentinck, of Foreign Office, 105

C.C.O., 108, 109

CELERY, 63, 73, 84; with SNOW in Lisbon, 90–92

Censorship, 87

199